Twice Widowed

"In the end, grief must be about becoming whole," Lorrie Fields says in the opening of *Twice Widowed*. Then, she narrates her journey into grief—a grief of deep pain catalyzed by the abrupt extinction of great love, two times. The reader is treated as a companion and close friend on this journey. Both joy and hurt erupt in full sensation; Lorrie finds words to express the inexpressible. She culminates her story with an awestruck encounter and exchange with mercy. You will be touched. Both my husband and I are lifelong friends of Lorrie and witnesses of her brokenness and steadfastness.

Patty & Mike Berens, PhD,
Public Speaker, Hospital Chaplain
Professor and Director, Cancer and Cell Biology

I (along with my husband) have been long time friends with Lorrie and her late husband, Darrell. We met in Hawaii in the 80s when our families lived there. I have walked much of this story with her. It's all true, gritty, raw, and visceral. In *Twice Widowed*, Lorrie writes in such a way that you will experience on every page the joy of living, spontaneous laughter, and the dark pain of loss. The amazing thing about this book is that not only is it a really great story, it is filled with grace, mercy, and the promise of healing for us all. This is a must read for everyone since grief and loss eventually come to most all of us. Lorrie's story will touch and encourage you.

Nancy Brown,
Commercial Real Estate

Twice Widowed is a deeply emotional book that grips our hearts and takes us on a journey from heartbreak to heartwarming. Lorrie is a masterful storyteller.

Beverly Scaggs

On life's journey, you rarely meet someone like Lorrie who is willing to go public with the most private travails of the soul. In *Twice Widowed*, Lorrie shows that she is a person who thinks through life. She wrestled with what it means to be truly authentic and what it means to be an example of meekness and humility, while at the same time purposefully engaged in the world. Lorrie's story needs to be told so that we can be encouraged by the victory that came when she wrestled with her faith, bitter disappointment, and doubt.

Cheryl and Quintin Frey,
Kroger Division President - retired

Twice Widowed is a firsthand look into the grief of Lorrie Fields's losses of two precious husbands, (including the accident that left her and her son injured) that took her to the depths of her soul. I love that Lorrie doesn't leave us in her sorrows but allows us into the process that enabled her to find courage to reconcile her fears. Her story is about how tragedy and sorrow are turned to joy. It is told in a vivid and compelling way. You'll see that joy is not about feeling happy, but about tangible inner peace and strength. I know Lorrie personally and can attest to the truth of her life and her victory. She proves the power of joy.

Deborah Keller,
Talent Acquisition

Lorrie Fields is an exceptional wordsmith. *Twice Widowed* will not disappoint. Every word, every sentence, and each memory so poignantly told played before me on a full-color screen with all my senses engaged. I don't think that I breathed much during those first pages. Her brave and raw honesty deepened my understanding of how important it is to not waste our grief. You will be a better human being because of this read.

Marie Umidi,
Writer, Director, and Producer

Wow! *Twice Widowed* is such a powerful book. Once I picked it up, I couldn't put it down. I was seated right next to the author's heart, laughing one minute and crying the next right down to the last sentence. It is a unique book of an authentic woman who has experienced more pain in a lifetime than most should. Yet, reading this one ends up believing that not only can you survive but even thrive after such tragedy. Not only is the story genuine and accurate (I have been a long-time friend), it is written with such excellence that you feel you are right there with her in life and death, through her travels from Hawaii to Europe, and through her despair and hope. I look forward to many more books by Lorrie.

Sam Scaggs,
Author and Consultant

TWICE WIDOWED

Coming into Wholeness
After Life Altering Loss

LORRIE FIELDS

NEW YORK

LONDON • NASHVILLE • MELBOURNE • VANCOUVER

Twice Widowed

Coming into Wholeness After Life Altering Loss

Published in New York, New York, by Morgan James Publishing. Morgan James is a trademark of Morgan James, LLC. www.MorganJamesPublishing.com

Proudly distributed by Publishers Group West®

Scripture quotations are from the Bible (New International Version) on Bible Gateway. https://www.biblegateway.com

Morgan James BOGO™

A **FREE** ebook edition is available for you or a friend with the purchase of this print book.

CLEARLY SIGN YOUR NAME ABOVE

Instructions to claim your free ebook edition:
1. Visit MorganJamesBOGO.com
2. Sign your name CLEARLY in the space above
3. Complete the form and submit a photo of this entire page
4. You or your friend can download the ebook to your preferred device

ISBN 9781636984582 paperback
ISBN 9781636984599 ebook
Library of Congress Control Number: 2024933877

Cover & Interior Design by:
Christopher Kirk
www.GFSstudio.com

Editor:
Carol Kay, PhD

Cover Photograph:
Carl Anderson
Hampton Roads Photography

Cover Hair:
Liz Darling
Darling and Dapper Studios

Cover Makeup:
Sarah Cowell
Sweet Face Makeup Artistry

Morgan James PUBLISHING Builds with... **Habitat for Humanity** Peninsula and Greater Williamsburg

Morgan James is a proud partner of Habitat for Humanity Peninsula and Greater Williamsburg. Partners in building since 2006.

Get involved today! Visit: www.morgan-james-publishing.com/giving-back

TABLE OF CONTENTS

*I dedicate this book to those
who have yet to turn their sorrows into joy
and also to those who kept me in their love until mine did:
my beautiful family and friends.*

FORWARD

L orrie and I began our friendship nearly forty years ago. I met her and her young family at church in Hawaii, and as I learned of her past, I was appalled. Your first husband died!! Your first baby was harmed in the same accident that also broke your back!! I couldn't believe that this beautiful, smart, lovely young woman had already experienced widowhood and terrible suffering such as I had never known or contemplated.

Over the years, I was involved with the Fields Family in so many wonderful ways. Darrell and I acted and sang together on our church's drama team. Our children played and homeschooled together. Lorrie and I developed a deep and abiding girl friendship as we shared our hearts about everything important. She was used to open my mind to the possibilities of the peace available to us— no matter the crisis.

And then my crisis came. Widowhood became my state of being at fifty-six years of age as I saw my husband leave for Heaven just a couple of years before Lorrie lost Darrell. It's been nine years of widowhood for me now, and Lorrie's book captures SO much of what we widows (and widowers) need to know.

Please read this book! It will enrich your life, widowed or not. Lorrie's intimate portrayals of her experiences allows us to see into the soul of one who has learned truths well beyond her years! She has gained wisdom that can benefit everyone who will read *Twice Widowed*. I stand in awe of Lorrie's ability to convey concepts about her inner journey and the overall human condition.

I thank you, dear Lorrie, for doing the hard work of writing this book and sharing yourself with all who will take the time to read it. I'm better for having known you and for having read this breathtaking book.

Tracy Yamamoto
Actress, Osaka, Japan
March 18, 2024

Dear reader,

Thank you for taking the time to read my deeply personal journey through widowhood. I have known many people with experiences far worse than mine. I have also met folks who think my story is incredible. They even add a disclaimer when telling me their stories: "It's not like what you went through." Before you read further, I want to say that loss is loss whether through divorce, finances, death, or tragedies untold.

These events affect our psyches no matter how they come into our lives. We all have to find a way to stay true to our best selves when navigating loss. That said, my experience became unique because of the layers of life events that complicated my grief and overwhelmed whatever strength I had counted on. I had to fight cynicism as if it were a naughty muse trying to dumb down my life. All I had along the way were my unvarnished feelings and beliefs—with all their coldblooded ups and downs, tormenting me as if I couldn't find wholeness. They were what I chose to write about. They were the mirrors revealing my broken soul that needed desperately to find peace. They were the journey.

I was intentional about sticking to the narrative of my story rather than trying to explain it. It seemed to me that trying to make it palatable, even for myself, was dishonest. I did change my point of view periodically when appropriate in the context, but I was keenly aware that instructing people who are hurting is mostly unhelpful. No one really knows the path, the truth, or the timing another person needs at any given moment. To those who are heartbroken, however, I hope that reading the following pages will somehow be my way of welcoming you to feel what you need to feel in a safe place of acceptance.

I wrote from a Christian foundation, even though I have been at odds with parts of Christendom for a long while (as you may see). Nonetheless, it has been my life from the time I was fifteen years old. I had to tell my reality from this faith perspective merely because it was my life. Sometimes it made things harder because there is no "que-sera-sera" to dismiss life events as if God didn't exist. I say this because everyone has to use the resources at hand and test them in real time; they have to be more than mere rhetoric in difficult moments. My resources were no different and required proving in all my parts—body, soul, and spirit.

Loss is a no man's land, where *everything* is tried. Finding our way to the open air of renewed truth for life may come in surprising ways but we know it when it happens because it shifts our perspective. Although it seems unfair to be forced to take an unwelcome journey through loss, it has the potential to make us the best and more true versions of ourselves by offering the transcendence necessary to know ourselves anew and be at peace in our worlds. That's the beauty of suffering. We don't have to live diminished lives forever as if hope were a thing of the past. There is more. Always more.

Thank you for trusting me with your time, which I recognize is your life. As you read, I send love for your journey.

-Lorrie

When I think of pain—
Of anxiety that gnaws like fire and
loneliness that spreads out like a desert,
And the heartbreaking routine of monotonous misery,
Or again of dull aches that blacken our whole landscape
Or sudden nauseating pains
that knock a man's heart out in one blow,
Of pains that seem intolerable and then are suddenly increased...
If I knew any way of escape,
I would crawl through the sewers to find it.[1]

---

1   Lewis, C.S. *The Problem With Pain.* (New York: The McMillian Company, 1947)
     93.

INTRODUCTION

My heart has burst twice in this life from being widowed: once in my twenties and then in my fifties. I was lit on fire by two beautiful men; then, I was dimmed by their absence. Nothing prepared me for the soul-gouging agony in the years that followed each death. My experience with mourning in the first round proved little relief during the second one—a benefit I wished were due. But that's just it; the idea of having paid suffering's final toll is a myth.

Every grief is a singular experience. It must be so, no matter how helpful "grief work" (Freud) and "stages of grief" (Kubler-Ross) may be for some in framing the experience of loss for everyday use. The journey is unique simply because the variables of life are unique and changing in real time. We bring to grief a soul in flux. The specific features of each relationship, circumstance, and experience come to bear with every sorrow we face. Knowing it's common to become disoriented after a profound loss doesn't prevent feeling lost—just as it is no relief knowing that a dry socket is normal after having a tooth yanked out.

The pain is fully there the very moment it arrives. There's nothing to ease it, however we may squirm. The disfiguring effort to stop it only prolongs the inevitable. Nor does it help to check off various phases from a list, as if they were a once-and-done thing. They "will be back," perhaps echoing Schwarzenegger's fateful voice. Those who think differently either have yet to experience a life-changing grief, or they are double-dealing their soul. Self-deception being the festering splinter it is, will crudely find its way to the surface by the very poison it creates, or else it will finish us. It's inescapable. I know.

In the end, grief must be about becoming whole. It will never deliver you to your former person. That person is forever altered. Grief can, however, introduce you to a brand-new self. The phases of being disoriented, then, become the important work of reorienting. The inability to accept what has happened tells us we must find our way to coherence. Being angry can be an important guidepost for finding peace. It all requires becoming as unassuming as we can be in whatever space we find ourselves. It requires letting go not just of our loved ones, but also the former mindsets and patterns once relied upon for making the world secure.

In the end, grief must be about becoming whole. It will never deliver you to your former person. That person is forever altered.

At times, we want to plead for mercy because we can't imagine being dissolved any further. Other times, we may torque the opposite way, toughing it out, as if having a stiff-upper-lip nullifies the obvious. Shutting down, becoming hyper-vigilant, or putting up smokescreens only means survival mode is in play. It's okay: those reactions keep us alive in acute moments. It's just that the more whole we become, the less we need those devices.

When I first thought about writing my journey through grief, I was navigating a dark period in the second year of widowhood in 2020. I had shut down for the first time in my life. My thoughts would not hold together; my memory was wrecked and my anxiety was off the charts. I first took notice of a shift toward insanity the day I hosted my father's Zoom memorial, nearly at the one-year mark of my second husband's death. I felt like a crazy person when a random phrase got stuck in my head, on repeat. All. Day. Long.

It was then that I put real effort into journaling, although at first, the effort looked like detached staring at blank pages. I had journaled after my first husband died too. Both times it felt futile. This time was worse. My words were as choppy on paper as they were in my mind. But I kept trying, thinking I might write myself back to me. I had hoped to discipline myself to think more succinctly and perhaps tap into those parts of me struggling to move forward. I thought staying with words until they stuck together could restore this brain of mine to what it had been—or maybe not.

Oddly, sometime toward the end of this dark period, the pressure eased, even though my circumstances were the same... even more daunting in significant ways. But I stopped trying to push away suffering. Rather, I incorporated it as the unrelenting and truly sacred reality that was justly mine. That's when I could relax into the unknown. It was like floating down a river blind. My senses tuned to different sounds altogether. The rhythm of my healing became a wonder—a terrible-beautiful adventure. I don't know what state of mind I will be in when I write the last chapter of this story. I am looking forward to knowing it—and to meeting myself there.

> The rhythm of my healing became a wonder—
> a terrible-beautiful adventure.

Ironically, I haven't written myself back to me but have, instead, scribbled myself forward. The inspiration from those journal pages is what follows here. At times, I still have trouble holding my mind on tasks. Situations can quickly become complicated. Symptoms of trauma periodically hazard my peace. The difference now, all these months later, is that I am kinder to myself. I fit into the world differently. Alone. Incredibly, the creative energy coming to me from the tension of suffering and belonging has paradoxically caused me to come alive in the wilderness. I no longer judge myself to be ill-suited for this wild and risky existence. It is life. It is my life.

NEVER ENOUGH

"It's been a year now since Dad died," Sarah, my daughter, said on April 23, 2020. My husband, Darrell, had left this earth in the morning exactly three-hundred and sixty-five days prior. The calendar was a jeering monster, a daily reminder of the reason for our torment. Sarah had clearly anticipated it to be so. The day Darrell left us, she said to me, "Tomorrow, we are going to say Dad died yesterday. And then we'll say, last month—and then, last year." I sighed, knowingly. This was my second loss of a great love. I knew the truth of the marked days and years ahead. I grieved that reality for her and with her.

The afternoon of Darrell's death the mortician had instructed us to pick out a grave plot. My children and I robotically drove to a cemetery in Norfolk to look for a resting place for Darrell's body. Before we arrived, someone suggested that we eat first. It snapped me back to reality. Food? Okay, right. We needed to eat after a day and a half of minimal food as we all watched Darrell fade away. Food wasn't on my mind, but I was still a mother. Their hunger quickened those instincts.

> How could I be true to myself, which was utterly wrecked, and be strong for them at the same time?

We gathered around a picnic table at Handsome Biscuit in Norfolk, marveling over the normal act of feeding ourselves on this highly abnormal day. It felt wrong somehow. Yet, this act sank to the ground the bubble we inhabited. I looked at my children while we lived and breathed separated from the world swirling outside of us. These precious souls were turned inside out. They were more beautiful and honest than ever before. The weight of wanting to lead them through this hit me as we ate our overstuffed sweet potato biscuits. How could I be true to myself, which was utterly wrecked, and be strong for them at the same time? How would I find hope, much less joy, in an uncertain future that I suddenly didn't want? I knew they'd be watching.

The kids and I decided weeks before this death anniversary that we would do a repeat of that meal, taking our biscuit sandwich order to Darrell's gravesite for a picnic. Jeffrey threw the blanket over the grass. I approached the headstone, engraved with a few of Darrell's last words as if I had been dragged there by an evil trafficker bent on exploiting my frailties. I wanted to feel differently. Two days prior, on what would have been Darrell's and my thirty-sixth wedding anniversary, I received shocking news: the foundation for my career path had been abruptly upended. The consequence seemed hostile to my singular purpose, which was to finish the work Darrell and I had started.

The news landed in me as one of the top ten worst experiences of my life, debatably at number seven. It jettisoned me backward, threatening the grief work yet to occupy my mind and heart. The soul needs quiet, peace, and safety to unveil its truth; I knew what consequence this news might have for me and those demanding I produce something marketable. I wrote it in my journal, fearing the judgment of others would turn into evidence for decisions being made that affected my future.

Additionally, being able to process Darrell's death had been postponed because of multiple life events that first year, which required me to keep my two dukes up, so to speak. It couldn't be helped. I genuinely tried to roll with my punches, earnestly trusting my fortitude. I danced around grief, knowing I would face its unforgiving digs whenever life stabilized. I remember the conversations I had had with myself during some of these events when my anguish nearly boiled over. "Not now," I would say as if my emotions were a separate entity. Crazy talk, I know. Then, by the time the next spring came after Darrell's death, I felt safe enough to give way to my grief—to go there—wherever "there" would take me. It felt permissible to drop my arms; but, by the end of April, they were up again.

I sat on Darrell's memorial bench, engraved with his last wishes for me and the children as if I were outside the moment meant for me. I thought I was disrespecting Darrell and our life together by being so removed. I finished my biscuit and stood, Darrell beneath my feet. I read the memorialized words carved in the granite: "I leave you joy." What. Was. He. Thinking? I squeezed my eyes and slightly shook my head, questioning his overly sympathetic wish. I couldn't find meaningful words to say to my kids, either. I wanted to, but I couldn't form them sincerely. Irreverently, I said something like, "Okay, we did it. Ready to go?"

> I danced around grief, knowing I would face its unforgiving digs whenever life stabilized.

Sarah didn't move; she looked longingly at me. I knew she was trying to discern my tolerance. Mindful of the likely visible angst on my face, I turned my lips upward. Sensing my willingness to stay, Sarah began to tell a story. She recalled the last song she and her dad had sung together. The two of them always had the unique ability to connect through song, both having beautiful voices. She had a moment in the car with Darrell singing the song "Never Enough", from the movie, *The Greatest Showman.* I remembered the song, but not all the words. "Can you sing it now?" I asked. She began quietly through tears, then powerfully. She sang about the moments one wishes to never end and how they steal your breath away. The song told about dreams realized and about worldly adventures and accolades. It spoke of gold, glitter, and the splendor of life but how those could never satisfy without a love to share them with.

My knees buckled as I absorbed the words. My pain vented forcefully. Random memories thrashed about in my soul: the dreams Darrell had set off in me, his magnificent role in them, how together we validated our story, how we were transformed by it. How vulnerable I felt without him. He would have eased the troubles of the last year, including the outrageous news I had received two days prior that struck at the core of not just Darrell's and my work but of my person. It made me feel as if my lover were being ripped from my arms all over again. Our work was where I found him still. I even bemoaned future successes when the reality of our vision would one day materialize, not a one could ever serve as consolation for the dreadfulness of living deprived of him now and forever. It could never be enough. I felt ruined all over again.

I draped myself over his memorial bench and quietly sobbed. These iced emotions were permitted to melt a bit by Sarah's song. I stayed there. After several minutes, I noticed that my tears were filling the hollows of the engraved words on his bench. How completely rude to be taken out of the moment, I thought, and by slobber no less. I didn't realize just how much I needed to feel them. But I also became aware of Sarah and Jeffrey, right there, crying with me and for me. I suddenly was uncomfortable relinquished to my feelings in front of them. I rose, hugged them both and kissed their tear-stained faces.

I wondered why that song was meaningful to Sarah. The words perfectly anticipated this day. What was its significance when she and her dad both sang it together? So, I asked. Sarah said, "Toward the end of Dad's being able to walk, we ordered takeaway for lunch. We sat in the car waiting for our food and sang "Never Enough". He also wondered what it meant to me. I told him how when I had first heard the lyrics, I unexpectedly had a picture of God, creating the entire universe. It wasn't enough. The earth and all its marvels weren't enough; he had to make me. I told him that I was the darling in the song. He needed me—the object of his affection. The Creator needed me."

Sarah caused me to wonder if I were still needed in creation. Thirty-eight years previous, after marrying my first husband, I knew I was. Life was exciting and full of promise. It was an adventure, and I enjoyed every minute of it.

LOVE GIVEN
AND TAKEN

I t was 1982. I was swaying to the music at church with my new-born son, Jeffrey, in my arms and my handsome husband—my first husband, Jeff, at my side. A tap on my shoulder interrupted my thoughts, an internal conversation echoing my sheer happiness. It was my friend, an older Greek parishioner, Sofia. She leaned into me and whispered, "You're glowing, Lorrie." Impulsively I replied, "It is SOOO true, Sophia," as if she were in my head too. But then, I thought to pull back my words. Perhaps I was a bit too self-possessed. Sofia smiled back knowingly, motherly. She let me keep that moment just as it was.

I first took real notice of Jeff Wade in the seventies as a teen when he cut off my Mom and me at the entrance to our high school in Lake Havasu City, Arizona. His souped-up, metallic gold, 1967 Mustang screeched into the parking lot as Mom dropped me off for pom-pom practice. "I would never date someone like that!" I said out loud. How discourteous Jeff seemed.

I knew who this boy was: a tall young man with a beaming smile and extraordinarily long eyelashes who had a promising athletic career and was actively scouted by universities throughout high school. His sister was a cheerleader on my squad. In the seventh grade, I went motorcycling with Jeff and other junior high classmates. That was my last spin on my Suzuki 250. I flipped my bike over that day and badly burned my leg. In a coming-of-age epiphany, I suddenly realized that unscared legs might be important to me when I would become a "woman" someday. To date, I hadn't. I was merely a flat-chested, long-legged, awkward girl who sometimes rode her motorcycle with the boys, and once with Jeff Wade.

I went to my first dance in high school with a guy named Mike. Our parents dropped us off at a local restaurant to meet up with another couple for a double date. The guy was Jeff—the good-looking rude boy I had forgotten about before now. Up close, Jeff wasn't anything like I had thought. He was funny, charming, and engaging. He doted on his date. They ordered burgers and fries. I was about to do the same when my date suddenly exclaimed, "I'll have cottage cheese." What the heck? I wondered if he had any money. I had some, in any event

My mind scrambled to know what to do. "Uh, um," I muttered behind my menu while trying to pick out something else to eat. Jeff's date pretended not to hear our waitress ask a if he wanted a side or a bowl of COTTAGE CHEESE! Jeff's face didn't show the same restraint. His grin nearly exploded into laughter. He peered over my menu and gave me a wide-eyed look of support. I put the menu down and said, "I'll have applesauce." Jeff threw his head back but knotted his shoulders to control his laughter. I smirked just for him to see. We shared a moment. Meanwhile, my date barely had a clue.

After dinner, we piled into Jeff's Mustang to drive to the dance. Jeff looked at me repeatedly through his rearview mirror. It made me nervous that our dates were going to wonder if Jeff liked me. I was wondering. Suddenly I was jealous of Jeff's hand holding with his girl. Jeff took us all home after the dance; but first, he stopped off at his favorite sub shop. The applesauce was long gone; I was starving. As we walked in, Jeff announced that he was paying. To this, Mike ordered a foot-long sandwich. I sized up Mike and ended our relationship the next day. However, it was the beginning of a whole new life with Jeff.

Jeff and I began dating after the double date. By my junior year, Jeff asked me to listen to a song as we sat in my driveway when he brought me home after our respective after-school practices. Some of the lyrics said, "I love the way you walk; I love the way you talk…" His eyes welled up as the song continued. He had me at "the way you walk" since I had been teased mercilessly growing up for having "swivel hip," and "parakeet legs." I looked at him judiciously. His affection entreated me to believe him. When he drove off, I squealed. I couldn't help it. Pure joy twisted me around on one foot to the mocking eye of one of my brothers in the front yard.

I remember thinking that I couldn't tell anyone we were getting married because no one would believe me. I was barely sixteen. But I knew. Jeff did too, but we didn't talk about it just yet. By my senior year, we did. He proposed before he left for college. No one questioned our youth—not our parents, our pastor, or our friends. Everyone was happy. I was the most.

We were married in 1979 and went off to Tucson, where Jeff had already been a student, playing baseball for the University of Arizona. I had a scholarship but decided on part-time school since one of us needed to work. Halfway through our first year of marriage, I had surgery to remove part of one of my ovaries. It was my second surgery for the same condition. I had this habit of growing suspicious, grapefruit-size cysts. We were told that if we ever wanted to have a family, it would have to be now. That was hard to hear. I wasn't even twenty years old and we had plans. After noisy disapproval from his father, Jeff decided to quit baseball to start a family. I tried to talk him out of it, but he was determined.

We moved back to Lake Havasu City, on the Colorado River, and built a new home for our upcoming family. After one heart-breaking miscarriage, we had a beautiful baby boy, Jeffrey, in the spring of 1982. He was perfect. Life was perfect. Our home was full of my husband's never-waning smile and loads of love. I thought our son's first word would be "precious" since his dad always kissed him, telling him how precious he was.

When our son was nearly three months old, we flew to Hawaii to show off our newborn son to my family living in Oahu. We were also celebrating our third wedding anniversary. My father had moved and started a business in the Islands after Jeff and I were married. It was while we were in Hawaii that Jeff decided to go back to school: this time to join the ROTC program, hoping to enter the Air Force as an officer. He was already a small craft pilot but wanted training to fly jets. When we left Hawaii, we were excited about our life as a family. We had a baby, were in love, and owned a home with equity. Life was good… but only for a few hours more.

We landed in California to begin our drive to Arizona. Halfway home, our car flew off the road. To this day, the memory of that event continues to evade me. Many assumed Jeff fell asleep while driving through the Mohave Desert. That still seems improbable since the last thing I remember was our sneaking a kiss after we passed a stop sign on the desolate road on which we were traveling. The sign was less than two miles from where we crashed. Our Pontiac Trans Am flew over a berm and flipped end over end before landing back on its wheels.

I know I was awake during the crash because I braced myself against the windshield, evidenced by the hefty diamond setting of my wedding ring bent completely to one side and by plenty of glass pressed hard into my knuckles. Jeffrey's car seat came loose from the seat belt, so he and the car seat slammed around during the crash and ended up wedged upside down behind me. His head had suffered a final whack against the floorboard. My husband was squeezed out of the car and crushed during one of the car's rotations. He died July 8, 1982, the day after our accident and the day after our wedding anniversary.

I repeatedly had to be told that I had been in an auto accident. I kept patting my belly, thinking I was in labor. I remember asking for a different maternity bed because its hardness was causing me more pain. Little did I know that I was strapped to a wooden board. It wasn't until the shock wore off that I finally remembered having a son. Jeffrey and his dad had been air-lifted to Phoenix, and I was told that I would join them as soon as a helicopter was available. The doctor at the hospital in the small town of Parker, Arizona said that both Jeffrey and my husband were going to be fine and were taken to Phoenix as a precaution. So, when the attending physician stood in the doorway to make his grim announcement, I was put right back into shock. Traction gear secured me to the bed as my back and pelvis were broken. I had to move my head to see through the pulley system. The doctor glared at me for several moments, then quickly said, "He's gone."

"Where did they take him?" I asked, thinking my husband had been moved to another hospital. "No," said the doctor, "He is dead." Then... the man just walked away. No one was there. My dad and stepmom, Joyce, were en route from Hawaii. My in-laws were in Phoenix with Jeff's body and my baby. My only partner was a crusty, next-door patient, insisting that I stop crying. "What's going on in there? Stop it!" he demanded. I stopped, but it didn't matter because sudden shock overtook me again.

No one informed me of the severity of Jeff's injuries. If I were asked whether his life-support should be turned off, I would have said no. At least that would have given me a second to process the catastrophe that was about to change my life. To make matters worse, I didn't see him at the mortuary or go to his burial because I was immobilized. The reality was that I never got to say good-bye. He was, in fact, just gone. The last thing I remembered after the doctor made his whip-saw announcement of my husband's death and before I entered a week of confusion was the question I had asked a friend, "How could God's grace ever be sufficient for THIS?" I couldn't imagine it.

I knew I had to get out of that hospital and reunite with my son. Perhaps what I was being told about him wasn't true either; and he, too, would soon be gone. I was terrified. I attended the memorial service for my husband the day after my release from the hospital, to which hundreds of friends and family came. My sister bought me a back-brace-accommodating dress in black with a ruf-fled, high neckline and little pink flowers all over it. Not cute, but who cared? I don't remember much of the service since I had been given a shot of Demerol at my in-laws' house before the service by my OB-GYN, who was also a family friend. I had also been given Valium and Percodan. I was in a foggy daze. Despite all that, the pain was still excruciating. I only remember two things from the service that day: 1) my husband's roommate was there from univer-sity and 2) a lyric from a song entitled "Home Where I Belong".[2]

After the memorial service, I was agitated at the seeming non-chalance of the world that continued to eat, drink, and be merry at the family dinner, where a crowd of out-of-town guests had gath-ered. All I could think about was Jeffrey. I didn't want to visit with anyone much less hear folks carry on as if life actually did continue. Some of the out-of-towners were happy-drunk. I stayed in the bed-room at the memorial dinner, excused for my injuries. In truth, I was just exasperated believing levity could be had by anyone. I pleaded with my father, "Please, Dad, get me out of here and take me to Phoenix. I need to be with Jeffrey." "You can't travel," Dad said, repeating the doctor's orders. "Then I will hire someone to drive me!" I countered.

I arrived at Saint Joseph's Children's Hospital with my father ten days after the accident. The neurosurgeon met us. Instead of immediately being able to see Jeffrey in the intensive care unit, I was pushed in my wheelchair into an empty conference room. The doctor wanted to prepare me for what I was about to see. I was lis-tening to him through a veil of frustration. Didn't he know none of

---

2   Pat Terry, *Home Where I Belong*, 1976.

what he was telling me mattered? I didn't care that Jeffrey was now blind and whatever else, I just wanted to hold my baby. I felt like I was a third-party witness to the unfathomable report the doctor rattled on about. "Six brain hematomas, skull fractures, broken ribs and collar bones, enlarged ventricles, optic nerve damage," he explained. But, these words floated away in the sterile room where we were meeting. None of them landed in my heart or mind.

> I didn't care that Jeffrey was now blind and whatever else, I just wanted to hold my baby.

Finally, I was wheeled into the bustling ICU past a row of other infant children also fighting for their lives. Then, there was Jeffrey—alive! Even though there was a bolt drilled into his forehead, tubes and wires surrounding his body, and a wall of beeping machines encircling his crib, I felt LIFE as though it had an atmosphere of its own. I gasped. It took my breath away to see Jeffrey. The space he occupied seemed warm and illuminated. The outline of his body was sharp and crisp against the air, as though a bright light shone only on and around him.

The nurse attending Jeffrey was writing some notes with one hand. In her other hand was a massive syringe for tapping Jeffrey's fontanel (the soft spot on the top of his head). It was a bright red mixture of blood and cerebrospinal fluid. She startled at my arrival as if she hadn't expected me or perhaps hadn't meant me to see how much blood was still draining from Jeffrey's brain. It didn't compute for me. He was alive.

I wanted to jump out of my wheelchair. "Please, may I hold him?" I asked the nurse. I knew he would be comforted to know that I was there after being without me all these horrific days. He needed to feel me, and I needed to feel him. I was told he had lost many of his reflexes. He couldn't even cry normally, just a little squeal. The nurse grimaced at my asking to nurse Jeffrey. I insisted on trying. It was an awkward ordeal to figure out the logistics of placing Jeffrey in my arms. We needed to pad my full-length, metal body brace which projected three inches off my torso while simultaneously keeping Jeffrey tethered to no less than five pieces of equipment. We looked like the Terminator mom and bionic baby, not the image likely to show up on baby card announcements.

Dad even helped by cutting two holes into an oversized t-shirt so I didn't have to take off my body brace to nurse. I looked ridiculous, but all that concern melted away at once when I touched my son's skin and felt his warm breath against my chest. All the shuffling of attentive nurses—all the sounds of heart and lung monitors and frequent alarms going off—completely disappeared in this dream world I had entered. After only a few seconds, I knew Jeffrey remembered me because he began nuzzling, just like all healthy babies do. Suddenly what flowed between us was more than physical nourishment.

We all cried at the sight of Jeffrey's nursing—the hospital staff, Dad, and me. I didn't even care that my father saw me in all my raw glory. It was a miracle and everyone knew it. Then something unfitting began to happen: music started to play in my head. I didn't want to sing. I kept trying to resist it. I had a conversation with myself to NOT think about the words that repeatedly found their way to the tip of my tongue, like an annoying jingle that gets stuck in one's head. Then suddenly, the meaning of the words set a stake in my mind. It startled me. I hadn't been paying attention. The song seemed to defy, or rather, mock reality.

Immediately I knew the implication and pleaded, "No, no, no!" The words were risky. Moments later the song would return. I considered it again with a sigh. Okay, so what if I believe these words and Jeffrey dies, anyway? What would happen to me and my faith? I was frightened at the thought, yet I couldn't deny the warm, comforting feeling settling all around me. It swept me in. Softly, through a new flood of tears, I began to sing to Jeffrey. I was cognizant of every word and the trouble it could become to believe them. They were from an old church hymn. What I remembered of it was this:

Sad hearts weep no more.
He has healed the broken-hearted,
opened wide the prison doors.
He is able to deliver evermore.[3]

Then, I dared to believe. I couldn't wait to take Jeffrey home, although it wouldn't be for three more weeks. I knew that he was going to live.

---

3   G.M. Mills, *His Name is Jesus*, a hymn (public domain).

YES TO LIFE

Janet arrived at my door two days after I had brought Jeffrey home from the hospital. She was Jeffrey's and my nurse, and a constant help during our recovery. She had come to live with me in the home Jeff had built for us after we had left university. My stepmom, Joyce, had taken Dad's place to be caretaker for Jeffrey and me, but she needed to return to Hawaii. Everyone, including me, knew I would need full-time help for a while. Joyce and I threw names out for the people who might be available. My in-laws, as well as my mother and stepfather, lived in my hometown and were all planning on shuffling me about. As incredibly loving as they all were, I wanted to have autonomy by living in my own home.

I thought of this lovely woman, Janet, who my husband knew well: she had played in a band with Jeff. She was an extraordinary choice because it seemed she was from a whole different planet. She was a New Yorker, an elaborate storyteller, the life of the party, an athlete, and familiar with fending off threats from the streets. While in the hospital with Jeffrey, I dismissed the thought of asking if she were available.

Coincidentally, back in Lake Havasu City, Janet had considered helping me, but she was planning on returning to New York after deciding that Arizona was not where she wanted to live. When her car suddenly needed major repairs, which depleted her moving-home money, she suddenly had the time. So, when Janet showed up at my door, Joyce and I were more than curious. She had no way of knowing what Joyce and I had talked about. When Joyce opened the door for Janet, she impulsively said, "It's you! We've been waiting for you!" Janet's eyes widened but she didn't blink. Janet fired back as fast as an auctioneer like she knew that any delay would set her feet to running. "I think I am being sent here to see if Lorrie needs help!" My eyes were now the ones popping out.

She moved into the spare bedroom. When we ate our first meal together, she felt perfectly comfortable licking her finger and with bird-like speed, pecking up every left-over sesame seed on *my* plate. I wondered if she had noticed how fast my eyes were blinking, or if she could hear me sucking in air. Nonetheless, Janet was perfect for Jeffrey and me. She was meticulous, compassionate, self-sacrificing, funny, and such a love. I let her eat anything off my plate whenever she wanted. I am certain that I learned to take the same liberties with her tasty bits. She made me laugh, even when I didn't want to. She also filled our home with music as her fingers danced across my piano's keyboard. I grew to love and trust her deeply.

Janet was my constant companion and my right arm for two years. When I needed to organize a community-based, neurological therapy program for Jeffrey, she did the scheduling and made sure everything was in order when people came to help. It took three people three times a day to perform the methods of recovery I had been taught at a brain injury institute.[4]

When Jeffrey was back in the hospital for surgery to insert a shunt into the ventricles of his brain, I would have to pump my breast milk so Jeffrey's fluids could be monitored to prevent seizures. Janet would go with me to what seemed like a commercial milking station in the hospital. It was all completely humiliating, feeling like a Jersey cow and all. Yet I was amply blessed. Even though I only pumped once a day, I would fill up 16 two-ounce containers. Every time, I was so embarrassed to come out of that room with all those bottles, so I covered them with a cloth. But Janet wouldn't have it. "Heck no," she said. "Give me that." She quickly uncovered the tray and bolted out of the room. She stuck out her chest as if she had just produced it all and proudly strutted through the hospital corridor like she had the antidote for world hunger or something.

During the first days in my home, Janet insisted on sleeping at the foot of my bed, putting a little bell on my nightstand, just in case she didn't hear me when I needed something. She would jump at the slightest sound Jeffrey would make to be sure I never had to lift him, change his diaper, or risk hurting myself since at

---

4   I can't leave this section of writing without lovingly acknowledging all those who heroically helped Jeffrey (and me) through his therapy: my mom, Laura, my mother-in-law Therese, my brother, Dan, my sisters in law, Joy and Joanne, and the vast number of community folks and friends in Lake Havasu City, AZ.

that time, I was just starting to walk again and still in a full-length body brace. Later she told me that she would sit at the door of my room and listen to my sobbing, praying for me when I woke up from another bad dream.

After two years, Jeffrey was catching up. He had regained his sight. His neurosurgeon finally believed my son could see when Jeffrey pulled the doctor's glasses off his head as he inspected Jeffrey's optic nerves. Jeffrey was creeping around and even began to walk. Janet and I took a break from Jeffrey's therapy and went to Hawaii for a holiday to stay with my family.

At dinner one night, my brother, Kevin, invited me to play beach volleyball. Uh, no, I thought. I was just now free of constant pain. Besides, it was a singles event. But before I could say anything, the entire table immediately chimed in at once. Joyce, Dad, and my other brother, Josh, all thought it sounded grand. "You should go. It will be fun," Joyce insisted. "I want time with Jeffrey," Dad added. Josh shook his head up and down in agreement with it all. It was as if they had schemed the idea of me getting out into the world. "Alright, I'll go but don't ask me to play."

Kevin and I walked onto Waikiki Beach, across from Honolulu Zoo, where volleyball nets are in perpetual use. Kevin jumped into a game already in play. I sat nearby, watching the tourists and locals. Sometimes I watched the game. I was uncomfortable. For the first time, I felt just how far removed I was from the norms of the world. Every day during the last two years was consequential, focused, and hard work. People playing around seemed trivial, although I knew it was entirely regular. Besides, in between sets, several couples were all kissy-faced. One of those was this muscular, curly-headed guy and his Hawaiian girlfriend. It annoyed me so much. It reminded me of my loss, a feeling I had learned to bury since my vigilance to help Jeffrey recover trumped all pursuits.

I reacted to my discomfort by taking a walk to obstruct the clumsy emotions turning over inside of me. I handily allowed a disdain to rise for these "immature" singles for whom I had little in common. I vowed not to attend other singles events, no matter the pressure from my loved ones, who sincerely only wanted me to move along in life. I went to bed that night worse for the activity. I fell asleep cynical about the world. What was there for me? Widow's groups? Those folks were my grandmothers. I grabbed Jeffrey out of his bed and put him next to me. At least I was a mother to this beautiful two-year-old.

The following day, we all got up to go to my parents' church, which held services in a hotel. I sat in the spacious rear of the ballroom with Jeffrey in his stroller. The music began to play. Up in the first row of the church was that guy from the volleyball game. He seemed so... free. His smile was constant. I watched him engage with everyone around him. He laughed easily and sincerely. His eyes were mesmerizing. A rouge thought flashed in my mind as I studied this young man. "If I were to marry again, it'd be someone like that." Stunned at my contemplation, I whipped Jeffrey's stroller around and darted out of the hotel. How do I uncreate those words? I could scarcely breathe. My heart fluttered fast.

The ride along Kalanianaole Highway back to my parents' home after church seemed extraordinarily long. I remember conversations in the car fading into the background. Flashes of sunlight through the trees lining the road softly touched my cheek as if the rays had feathery wings. The road spoke as the tires passed over the asphalt. I could feel my body taking up space in the atmosphere. I was so aware of myself and my place alone on the earth. It was a curious moment but ironically soothing, almost like being given permission to occupy attention.

Once home, Janet put Jeffrey down for a nap after his favorite lunch of peanut butter and banana sandwich. I went straight outside to dangle my legs over the dock in the backyard. My parents lived at the water's edge on a bay that leads out to the open ocean. It was a favorite quiet-time spot for everyone, nestled underneath several swaying coconut trees and overlooking the east end of the Ko'olau Mountains as they eased their way down into the Pacific ocean.

My emotions didn't take long to rise as steep as those Ko'olaus. Then, they crashed down in one sharp gasp. I was powerless to talk myself out of it. My eyes were streaming tears, but I wasn't sobbing. It was like a pressure valve was released inside me, bypassing my mind at first. I suspected it had to do with my husband and was provoked by the mystery man I didn't know but had seen twice.

My family dismissed my isolation that day. I wanted to talk less and less about my feelings as time passed, and it was good no one had tried. I was at odds with words, anyway, since the excess of them seemed to nullify the power of the most important ones. Everyone talked too much, even me. By now I had heard plenty of explanations about why a person must die. The worst reason was that Jeff's beliefs were wrong, so God could not let him live. Some wanted to dumb down my grief by comparing losing a husband to losing a parent. To this person (who had never lost a spouse), losing a parent was the worst since mothers and fathers can't be replaced. Instead, she said, "You can get a new husband, Lorrie." Right, I thought, like from a catalog or something.

I was at odds with words, anyway, since the excess
of them seemed to nullify the power of the most
important ones.

Then there were ideas floating around that Jeff was so pure that
God needed him in heaven. I bristled repeatedly at that surprisingly common suggestion. No, No! God didn't. He's God after all.
He had Jeff's devotion here. Perhaps these ideas of a divine need
for souls were gratifying news in a different universe than the one
tightening around me. But, in mine, Jeffrey and I would be forever
changed from our injuries to both our bodies and souls. Jeff may
have only experienced death for a few moments, but I was living it
daily. Now, how was I going to live here without him? How was I
going to take care of Jeffrey by myself? How could I move forward
with anything or return to school as planned? No, I was certain I
needed Jeff more.

My response to those attempting to help me move along was
merely a slight smile. They were being nice apart from how tone-
deaf their words sounded. There are bits of life that cannot be
explained outside of experience. My popping off to inform their
opinion would set everyone on their heels. It would have been a
completely pointless use of spare energy. Besides, moving forward
felt wrong no matter how many exhortations to do so played in my
ears like a broken record. I couldn't explain that to anyone.

The wrestling in my heart on the dock essentially put my vow to
Jeff up against another romantic relationship with anyone, including curly-head, with whom I had only ever exchanged a glance. In
the deepest parts of my soul, letting go of my past and my suffering seemed like voiding my life altogether. I didn't think I could

do it. Overwhelmed with the prospect of a new relationship, but strangely and suddenly at rest, I pulled myself together enough to go back into the house. I fell fast asleep.

> In the deepest parts of my soul, letting go of my past and my suffering seemed like voiding my life altogether. I didn't think I could do it.

The next week was easy. I gave myself the benefit of the doubt for the Mexican stand-off I was having with myself and perhaps God. I dismissed the way-too-serious dialogue going on in my head. Janet and I took Jeffrey to the zoo and the beach. We went shopping at the Ala Moana Mall: we were the quintessential tourists. At a cultural show, Janet even got kissed by a painted, half-naked Maori dancer. Then my brother rerouted my attention; he invited "the guy" over to the house for dinner and to watch a movie. What the heck? The thought of it unmoored me. What if he tried to talk to me... alone?

"This is Darrell Fields," my brother, Kevin, said looking at me with a bit of tomfoolery in his eyes. "This is Lorrie Wade, my sister," Kevin continued. I stared motionless at Darrell. He arrived at the house wearing a black aloha shirt tucked into white drawstring pants. Now I could see those eyes up close. They were piercing light blue with gold rings around his pupils. He wore his dark, curly hair parted in the middle, touching the nape of his neck. He was hotness personified and persisted in being that engaging man I had imagined he was at church. He seemed unaware of how weaponized his charisma was. I tried not to let my new resolve become neutralized, but, it did.

The whole family gathered to watch the movie Blue Thunder. I had seen it on the plane and loved it. What I didn't know was that the plane version had been edited. So, when the unedited romantic scenes began, I was embarrassed to be sitting next to Darrell. There was unspoken tension lingering even after those scenes.

The last time I thought about my sexuality was when a married woman asked me what I was doing about my "desires" since Jeff had died. It stunned me for two reasons. First, the meddling nature of the question itself. Second, I hadn't entertained the thought, not once, until the moment she said it. "Nothing!" I replied, turning my eyes away quickly, envisioning her supposed solution. My husband was dead, so what was she asking? I didn't want to sully my memory or myself. The beauty of Jeff's and my intimacy went far beyond the encounter she had suggested was a necessity. Growing up I met a few carnal brutes; a fact I wished I had never encountered. Once I had, I developed a radar for men looking for mere hookups.

In my first year of widowhood, a man I had known, pretending to help me when I was out on an errand, randomly announced, "I'd take you if I weren't married." I ran out of the building after he had started kissing me down my neck when he thought no one was around—and after I jarred myself free from an initial shock paralysis. If I were to give myself in that way ever again, it would spring from the kind of intimacy that says, "I feel safe with you." So, "take" me? Yeah, NO! No one would be taking me or helping themselves to gifts not given.

Yet, something was awakening in me with Darrell sitting nearby. I felt vulnerable when my family went to bed (on cue, it seemed) and left Darrell in the living room with me. How was he going to get home? Was I going to have to drive him? Then on second thought, I was pleased to have him stay. We didn't need any lights on in the house that night since the bright, full moon shone through the sliding doors and surrounded us as we sat on my parents' plush white sofa. It was admittedly romantic.

Darrell wasn't threatening. He was so easy to talk to, although I became distracted trying to fit his name to his person. Who was I looking at? He was a man's-kind-of-man, with strong hands and developed muscles. But the name Darrell just didn't seem to work. For a minute I was busy trying out a slew of manlier names on Darrell. Perhaps Mark, Joe, or Scott would do. Something with just one syllable suited him better. Then again, he was pretty to look at, so Darrell (which translated in Hawaiian means "beautiful eyes") was probably the right name after all.

I scolded myself into listening again. I hoped that I didn't look as distracted as I was. I jumped back into the conversation that hadn't stopped while I was preoccupied thinking about names. Darrell continued telling me about his life, his move to Hawaii, and his family back in Washington and Montana. Then he asked me about mine as I sat near him with my feet curled underneath me. After telling him part of my story, I got nervous and flatly announced that I didn't think I could marry again. My random stiff-arming wasn't warranted in the moment, yet Darrell replied generously, "I don't think I could either if I were you." His eyes glistened saying it. Then he began to tell me how sorry he was for my loss. Wait, wait, wait. Don't go being all nice, I thought, while quickly raising my defenses once more.

"Well, you better go home now. It must be after two in the morning," I declared, vaulting up in haste to change the subject and find the car keys. I looked out the window: the light was different now. I could see sunlight slowly creeping across the bay. I ran to the kitchen to see the clock. It was nearly six o'clock in the morning; we had talked all night. I covered my mouth and dashed into my parents' room, leaving Darrell dumbfounded on the sofa. I don't know if I wanted to excuse myself for Darrell still being there or announce my achievement for enjoying conversing with a member of the male species. Darrell was their idea, anyway, so I thought they'd be sympathetic.

I could see sparkles in Joyce's eyes, as any mother might display thinking her child was finally moving forward. Dad halfway grinned but more in deference to Joyce's approval. I could see red flags in his furled brows. He was fighting not to rain on my parade. Nonetheless, he exhorted me to take Darrell back to his own home immediately. Before Darrell and I parted, he kissed me on the forehead. I felt it in my toes.

The next week Darrell called. We arranged a couple of outings. I wasn't going to call them dates. We went to Hanauma Bay. We had a blast snorkeling and sitting on our bamboo mats in the snowy, white sand. We talked easily and watched the contented world around us. Strangely, I felt like a welcomed guest in the happiness surrounding me. It was remarkable to feel a part. In the shrubbery that grew to soften the space between the sand and the inside walls of the crater, the mongooses danced, played, and stuck their heads out like busybodies spying on us and all the vacationers from around the world.

One day, Darrell and I went to Sandy Beach to body surf, which I had never done. It wasn't the best idea since I was mindful of my recently healed vertebrae. I would be a good sport nonetheless and at least get in the water. Darrell took my hand to lead me into the surf. I smiled back at him; he seemed thrilled to share this moment with me. We strolled to the edge of the white water and kept going. I was getting more nervous the farther we walked because walls of water popped up as instantaneously as they crashed, due to the way the ocean floor dropped off at this beach. It's the nasty reason Sandy Beach is well-known for neck and back injuries. Surely Darrell knew how far we could go. Besides, I was a good swimmer if we got out too deep—plan B. I trusted him. But what I hadn't learned about Darrell yet was that if you looked more critically at that satisfied expression on his face, just like the one that seduced me into following him into the water that day, you could detect the twinkle in his eyes that signaled when his soul was ripe for mischief. It was a habit that followed him to his last breath.

Suddenly he let go of my hand! In a flash, I saw his toes disappear into a wave just before it crashed on my head. There would be no breaststroke, no diving, not even a doggy paddle for me. I was suddenly helpless in a tangle of legs and arms as the ocean's violent sand-filled bubbles thrashed me about. When I bounced off the ocean floor, I thought I was going to drown. I finally knew I would live when I skid, face first, into the sloping shoreline. My body followed with a hard thud. My hair was flipped from the base of my neck, my head low just enough to cover the pieces of me now on the outside of my suit. When I finally composed myself on all fours, the roar of Darrell's laughter stuck me like a knife and grew even louder when I righted myself on two feet. Besides being layered in sand over every inch of my body, a wad of it somehow found its way into the lining of my bathing suit. It bounced when I walked to our beach mat.

It took me a while to get over that incident. I don't like bullies. Was Darrell one? Was he just ignorant, immature, or what? At least my back didn't hurt anymore. His feeling bad helped, but I wondered if I had made a mistake trying to be friends with him. Yet, I couldn't stop thinking about this beautiful man.

The following days were strange because I stopped being able to eat. I thought I must be going through some emotional trauma. Was Darrell to be in my future? At times, it felt like I was betraying myself and my marriage; I was still wearing my wedding ring. Joyce and I concluded that is why I felt sick. I was confused and lovesick, that's all.

Okay. I knew I had to step back so I could steady myself in this new paradigm. I didn't see Darrell for a week. I decided to return home earlier than later. I made plans, but I woke up one morning with a high fever and severe abdominal pain. Joyce drove me to the hospital to find out our self-diagnosis of lovesickness was not at all close to reality. I had a large ovarian cyst. It ruptured, spilling poison into my belly. Had I not been so out of sorts about Darrell I would have recognized my symptoms since I had had this malady twice before. The next thing I knew, I was in the operating room.

I woke up to Darrell singing. It was angelic, comforting… and weird. Why was HE there? Joyce had to work, so she brought him thinking it might be what I wanted. She was wrong. I was embarrassed being in a thin hospital gown and catheterized. Nonetheless, there was a remarkable peace flooding the room. When the anesthesia wore off, I was finally able to focus clearly. I remember looking quizzically at Darrell when suddenly it felt right that he was there. Oddly, it was like he had always been in my life. If he could only sing to me like this forever, I thought. We felt an otherworldly connection that we both wondered about then... and later. The hospital staff had removed my jewelry before surgery. I never put my wedding ring back on.

Darrell hinted about marriage, but I always changed the subject or pretended not to catch his drift. It had only been a few months of knowing each other. Yet, I found myself daydreaming about what it might be like to be married again—to Darrell. Once, Darrell was more forthright, but I rebuffed him, nicely, by saying, "Ask me again someday." There was no doubt we were developing a connection. I knew he adored Jeffrey. It was, however, a huge ask to give myself fully to the relationship when I was still trying to navigate widowhood.

One day, I had let the conversation go there—to marriage. Darrell did most of the talking. It was easier for him to imagine our being together than it was for me even though I was falling in love, BUT... I had lots of buts. We talked about them. There was my home in Arizona. Then there was the idea that I may not be an ideal candidate for a free-spirited man like Darrell, a fact Darrell argued well against. And there was his family. I hadn't met them. It broke a relationship rule I thought was important: to see a potential match in a family and friends dynamic. Suddenly, Jeffrey saved me from these disquieting topics.

"Jeffy, Jeffy poop," my two-year-old announced in the middle of our talking points. Whew! Before I could react to Jeffrey, Darrell scooped him up and ran to the bathroom. It was instinctive on his part and somehow consoling.

We decided to take Jeffrey to the zoo shortly after our more in-depth conversation about the nature of our relationship. Somehow, I could ease better into the moving forward part of life now.

Many of my previous rebuttals to the argument fell away. But there was just one more. "What would I wear?" I wondered out loud. "Now we finally reached the root of the problem," Darrell laughed.

I carried on ad nauseam to Darrell about what might be appropriate colors to wear for a second wedding (a perplexity that no longer exists in this century). Darrell placated me with mm-hmms and platitudes about dress colors. I said, "I know. I want to wear clear pink… if I were to ever get married again." "What's clear pink?" Darrell asked as we turned a corner. Right there was a tree (a pink Tecoma) in full bloom, so covered in blooms that hardly any green showed. It showed off the lightest, clearest pink flowers.

"That! It's that color," I said, suddenly gobsmacked. I stood, trying to shrink the coincidence, but I couldn't. The tree stole my breath. It bloomed the exact delicate pink I had seconds before been trying to describe. My eyes welled with tears in hope, or perhaps in embarrassment from foolishly being taken in by the oracle of a tree. Yet I wanted to suppose it bloomed just for me at that moment. We continued along our path when a breeze caused showers of pink blossoms to rain down on our heads. "You know that question you asked me?" I said, pausing to look at him. His eyes were already on fire with anticipation. "Yes. I say, yes!"

GRIEF BECOMES
MY FRIEND

Darrell took the microphone from the officiant and began to sing the "Hawaiian Wedding Song" to me while the dancers from the Don Ho Show did the hula at our wedding ceremony. The intended romance was ruined by Darrell's sweating profusely once he watched me walk down the aisle. By the time he sang the song's first note, beads of sweat were forming and dripping off the tip of his nose onto the mic. I felt sorry for him, but what I was more thinking about was how odd it was to sweat from one's nose.

Mostly, the day was undone by Jeff's mother, Therese, and my sisters-in-law sitting in the second row. It's not that Therese wasn't like a mother to me. She was. She taught me so much about life,

being a woman, motherhood, and more. She even made my wedding dress when I married Jeff. I loved her dearly. But her presence unnerved me, making me feel like I was betraying Jeff. I nearly became a run-away bride that day, even forming the words I would tell Dad about why I would be fleeing the chapel.

The wedding suddenly felt like a big mistake. I knew Dad wouldn't talk me out of whatever I decided last minute. Yet, I didn't say a word, wishing he would notice my conflict and initiate my escape. But he didn't, and when the music began I walked past my family from Arizona filled with regret. I just wanted to go home with them and forget the last months.

I had a dreadful time at the reception. If it weren't for Darrell going out of his way to reach out to my in-laws, they surely would have felt unwelcome. Perhaps they did, anyway. I feared I had already offended my sisters-in-law for mistakenly forgetting to have corsages made for them. Yet, Darrell covered for me. He encouraged them to visit anytime and talk about Jeff as much as they wanted. Darrell believed Jeffrey needed to know his father and the Wade family. It was a relief that Darrell was so gracious since I couldn't engage with my in-laws because of the guilt raining down on me.

How could I love a living man when I was in love with a dead one? That wasn't fair to anyone. I was an imposter.

Our wedding night was dreadful. I stayed in the bathroom, saying I needed to take a bath—a very long bath. Truthfully, I was sobbing as the water ran until I finally allowed the tub to fill. I had ruined everything, I thought. How unfair to Darrell. It was too soon for me. I tried to remember the connection Darrell and I had had, but I couldn't help knowing that I was connected to Jeff too. How could I love a living man when I was in love with a dead one? That wasn't fair to anyone. I was an imposter.

Three days later, we left the island and traveled to Montana and Arizona for two more receptions with family and friends. I was feeling somewhat better by the time we had arrived in Montana. Darrell was so proud to show Jeffrey and me off to his family. Once in Arizona, that pretender-me was back. Again, Darrell drew the focus away from me. He was magnanimous and kind to all my friends and family, who were meeting him for the first time. To those who presaged my mourning period over, it appeared that they were correct.

My Arizona house had sold while we were in Montana. The escrow closing coincided with our wedding reception in Lake Havasu City. It went off smashingly. Darrell sang beautifully—no longer sweating like a wrestler—and thanked the congregation for all they were to me, declaring his love and commitment to Jeffrey and me. People cried. I will never forget my stepfather, Jerry, crying behind the video camera while lovingly looking at me through the camera lens.

No one knew how tormented I was since stepping back into Jeff's and my home with Darrell two days prior. The first night sleeping there, Darrell jumped into my bed without regard. I saw Jeff lying there, fading in and out of the space Darrell occupied. When I stood paralyzed at the foot of the bed, he suddenly understood. Darrell rose from the bed with concern clearly on his face. He approached me but said nothing. Touching my shoulder, he smiled sweetly as he left to sleep in the guest room.

I wished I could have believed Darrell was mistaken…that it wasn't about Jeff, but I couldn't. I didn't know what to do. I climbed into Jeff's and my bed alone. I didn't cry, but I felt pain undulating in my gut. I felt my heartbeat increase and my breath cut short. Suddenly, I flew out of bed and ripped off the linens as if I were cursing them from ever providing comfort again. I sat hard on the chest at the end of the bed, the one Jeff had made for me. The heaviness I felt wanted to send me to the ground. Before it did, I darted into the guest room and crawled into bed next to Darrell. He rolled onto his back matching my position. He reached for my hand and held it until we fell asleep. Not a word was spoken.

We arrived back in Hawaii and moved into a condo on Oahu. We bought a new mattress, free of my haunts. Darrell, Jeffrey, and I slept on that mattress on the floor, camping out until my household arrived from Arizona. The empty space in the condo was a playground for Darrell and Jeffrey. I watched in wonder as the two of them played, giggled, and wrestled. Darrell truly loved him. When our things arrived, we realized that many items from our Matson container had been stolen. Of greatest significance, our electronic equipment and all our family videos were missing. The videos of Jeffrey and both my weddings' videos had all been lost. Darrell hadn't seen me fall apart until then. I plopped myself down in tears, exposing the underbelly of my fragile state of mind.

The following week Darrell was back to work as a draftsman. Jeffrey and I had our first real downtime with no therapy. We explored the zoo and the beaches. Jeffrey took his first swim lessons. I still felt out of sorts in my own skin, but I didn't know what it meant. I was increasingly frustrated at just being myself, by relearning me. Activities seemed unimportant and I couldn't figure out why.

I started to feel ill. Days of nausea turned into weeks. I made an appointment with the same doctor who performed my surgery when Darrell and I were dating. The symptoms, minus the fever, were similar to when that cyst had ruptured. After an examination and blood tests, the doctor gave an inconceivable diagnosis. "Congratulations," he said, "you're pregnant." I was stunned. I was told Jeffrey's conception was likely a singularity.

We bought our first home in Kalama Valley on the east end of Oahu a few months before our new son was born. Ten months into our marriage, our son arrived. I was happy to have the privilege of being the mother of another beautiful human being, Brian Anthony. Yet, there was another side to me, a disconnected side. It showed up subconsciously at first.

I was tortured by two recurring nightmares. The first nightmare: my husband, Jeff, and I would be speeding toward each other in a magnetosphere above the earth, like charged energies eager to collide. All life and light were below us in a surreal and cold space. I had to be strong and ready to grab him since Jeff's arms were bound so he couldn't help. Reaching, straining, and swimming through space, I finally reached him. But, he was suddenly whisked away just as our heads touched. I watched him grow smaller and smaller until he had disappeared. I lost him. I knew it was forever and I knew it was all my fault.

The second nightmare was just as horrifying. Jeff shocked me by showing up in perfect health at Darrell's and my home. He arrived in a red convertible, looking every bit like Cary Grant's film double. He was detached and angry. He wouldn't let me explain that I thought he was dead, or I would have never remarried. Apparently, he had been put on an island for severely disabled patients. My family kept the secret, so I could move on with my life. But Jeff miraculously recovered and came to Hawaii to find his son. He felt betrayed that I hadn't waited for him. To make it even more punishing, he and Darrell became good friends and decided they would raise the boys together. I had to leave. Forever. Just as I was driving away from both my husbands and my sons, I would wake up. It rattled me to my core.

The lack of coherence inside of me began to feel physical. I started losing weight too fast after my pregnancy. I barely had enough milk to nurse my new son. Slowly, I lost energy; my joints, my skin, and my muscles all hurt. When I got down to 104 pounds, Darrell insisted I go to the doctor. It turned out I had developed lupus. I look like my paternal grandmother, who also had lupus, so perhaps a genetic factor was involved. After the diagnosis, we hired a maid. She cleaned, cooked, and watched over Jeffrey so I could rest when Brian was asleep. My life was reduced to the bare minimum.

One weekend, Darrell decided to finish unpacking. He pulled book boxes from the garage and piled them near the bookcases that lined the window. One box held my journals from when I was first widowed. Some entries were written as letters to God, where prayers were easier to write than speak out loud because, for some odd reason, I was afraid of being disappointed if I didn't get a direct response. Darrell knelt next to me and started rifling through my journals. He was looking for anything displayable. "There is nothing in there," I coarsely said to Darrell's quizzical face. Those journals threatened me as the penny did for the time traveler, actor Christopher Reeves, in the movie, *Somewhere in Time*. Reeves pulled a forgotten penny from another time out of his pocket. The power emanating from his life in another dimension violently ripped him from the space he was occupying with his new lover, sending him tormented back to the future.

"Can we just tape them back up and put them in the closet?" I implored, like hurry up already. But Darrell kept rifling through the box. Picking up one of my journals, he asked if he could read it. The enormity of my suffering and the rawness of it was on those pages. Only God and I knew what was in there. Any grief accomplished during the years after my first husband's death was on full display. There was little time for sorrow in those days because I was consumed with recovering the quality of Jeffrey's life. I didn't speak about it.

Not many felt comfortable talking about Jeff anyway. I think some people, especially family members, didn't engage out of fear of upsetting me. I understood. Others didn't bring it up, prompted by a faith tradition that chides weakness. Several people claimed messages from God about my state of being, which were most irrelevant, often too prescriptive, and just plainly dismissive.

I surrendered to Darrell's sincerity but also to a desire for him to know me—the real me. I watched Darrell read page after page, wiping his tears as he went. I was crying too by then. Darrell's responsiveness was not tinged with jealousy. It wasn't just about my losing Jeff. Darrell and I connected on a more profoundly human level than ever before. When he finished reading several journals, he wrapped his hands around mine as he sat at my feet, looking carefully into my eyes. He began saying things like, "I am so sorry this happened to you" and "This should have never happened" and "He was such a wonderful person" and "I wish he never died."

I heard more than Darrell's words as he spoke. I believed him. Once I did, the trickle of tears turned into a waterfall. "Really, you think that?" I asked, crumbling in agony as if something was being torn from my soul. He held me until my sobbing subsided.

Lifting myself off his chest, I asked, "How can you say you wished he never died? We would never have met." He answered, "But you would never know that. You and Jeffrey would never have suffered as you have."

That moment of honest grief was inexplicably liberating. I never had another nightmare about my first husband from that day forward. I finally said goodbye to Jeff, my first love, the love of my youth, and my greatest, kindest friend. Additionally, I started to feel better. The doctors thought the lupus was in remission. Soon, I was back to good health, no longer needing a maid, although I kept her for a bit longer… just because. I knew I could finally move forward in confidence as my authentic self.

Grief had become my friend.

BEING ONE

The next ten years of our marriage were defined by growth—the stretching, the agonizing, and the liberating kind. Darrell adopted Jeffrey so he could be legally and fully his. We made many of our life-long friendships in those early years of marriage in Hawaii. We lived in a culture of hospitality, adventure, and travel. We learned that we could fight, embrace pain from wherever it came, and find all the healing we wanted. Our struggles fast-tracked our journey to a beautiful marriage when growth meant not having to defend a mistaken posture. We tried that "don't-see-my-faults thing" a time or two (or on repeat for a bit); but defensive, critical, and moody people don't find harmony with others, so we quit that and let ourselves become more and more vulnerable.

Darrell and I were practical jokers, always trying to outdo each other. Once, I painted Darrell's toenails pink in the middle of the night, only completing one set of toes because I was sure my muted laughter and jiggling the bed would wake Darrell. It was payback for his uninvited "pedicure" painting of my entire bare foot with house paint.

Miraculously we had another baby, our beautiful Sarah. Again, I thought I couldn't get pregnant. So, when I started feeling excessively fatigued, I went to the doctor for tests to see if that sinister lupus was back. Darrell, remembering my illness, was more nervous than I was about the results of the tests. The phone call came after I was back home. Darrell watched me speak to the nurse from outside the sliding glass door where he played with the boys. Relentlessly, he studied me through the glass. Darrell rushed inside the house when I appeared stunned by the conversation. "What?" he insisted. Unable to answer at first, I just began laughing. Finally, I said, "She said my hCG was high." "What does that mean?" He demanded. "She said that we are pregnant."

I dreamed of having a girl, but in every sonogram the sex of the baby was undiscoverable because of how she lay in the womb. The day she was born, Darrell jumped up and down repeatedly saying, "It's a girl. A girl." He cried more than our newborn daughter, Sarah. I had a complete hysterectomy three years later when my one remaining half-sized ovary finally quit on me.

After Sarah was born, I kept my pregnancy weight for months. No mother was ever so happy to be fat following a pregnancy than me. Our family felt solid. I was irreversibly and wholly me, no longer the imposter I had felt myself to be. Motherhood was a natural fit for me and the best fun I ever had.

For the next twenty-some years, we were in Christian ministry together. It started as a dream for both of us. In the beginning, Darrell was passionate, inspired, and his best self. I was too. The demands and challenges pulled gifts we didn't know we had. I loved to hear him speak. I swooned when he sang in public. We were partners in every way, carrying the load of ministry together. Those years are worth another story, but I only want to mention them briefly as they played heavily in my future grief.

We moved to South Central Pennsylvania in 1995 for our first senior role in a church. It oddly felt like coming home when we stepped onto the ground in Pennsylvania, even though it was a different cultural ecosystem than we were used to. This was no criticism. We were merely curious after arriving in Pennsylvania about what appeared to be a guarded, even forbidding, response to our being in the state. It was a challenge to understand.

My young daughter, Sarah, called a grandmotherly Pennsylvanian, "Momo." She heard other children use that word. Sarah conflated the address with the aloha gestures we were used to. In our Hawaiian life, everyone older was either aunty or uncle. The woman immediately pushed back, squeezing my daughter's shoulder while sternly saying (and first looking at me as I hadn't taught my daughter properly), "You shall call me Mrs. Putman. Only my grandchildren call me Momo." Then, two people in the church separately interrogated us. "Why are you here? We were here first," they bemoaned to our astonishment.

There was the time when Darrell and I were in a boutique listening as the shop owner was grilled by a self-confessed elite, "You need to remember who I am. My family has been in this town for generations." Plenty of folks didn't cross into other townships, and they dared not cross the rivers. We jokingly wondered how some of them ever got to Philly for an authentic cheese steak. One time,

I mentioned this from the podium at a speaking engagement. The instant eruption of laughter made it clear that what was worrisome to me was perfectly customary. I also remember being stunned at reading a clause in a lease we signed. It said the property couldn't be rented to black people. When I questioned it, the realtor said it was an outdated form and didn't mean anything. Yet, it wasn't alarming enough for him to discontinue its use. Already we had seen how the different ethnic groups lived separated. Even my children noticed. Once, Brian had been thinking about this and wondering why he only saw white people everywhere. Perhaps he wondered how he fit in when from the back seat of the car he asked, "Mom, were Chinese, right?" Of course, we are not but he began life in Hawaii where colors blend in a spirit of aloha.

We might have brushed it off had these curiosities been isolated incidents, but they weren't. Within the first couple of months, we realized that we needed to know more. We couldn't take the folks' skepticism personally. How could we? No one knew us. What it did do, however, was drive us to inquire about the history of the area to understand the mindset of the people we were there to serve. Darrell accidentally ran into the life of William Penn while studying. Penn's contributions to forming the United States and his plan to include Native Americans in his government were extraordinary. It was the prooftext for the civil liberties he imagined as a fundamental operating principle for government, perhaps summed up with his quote, "We must give the liberties we ask."

Eventually, our curiosity turned into a book (with my help once I was happily co-opted into the project) entitled *The Seed of a Nation, Rediscovering America.* In it Darrell coined William Penn as America's first founding father. We saw similarities and contrasts in the mindsets of the colonists and today's Americans. More importantly, we grieved over lost potential because misrepresenting a strictly invitational gospel was not "good news"[5] at all. It required the free air and untidy love that allowed people not to choose. William Penn had a lot to say about this as a road to peace. His principles of the separation of church and state, religious liberty, and civil equality were critical to his prescription for any successful state. He was called "the greatest lawgiver the world has produced" by Thomas Jefferson (Thomas Jefferson's Draft Letter Nov. 16, 1825) but to Penn the law was only an expedient against the human default that robs others of their self-determination.

Darrell and I traveled around the state, speaking to whoever would listen. Once, when Darrell was speaking in Central Pennsylvania, a local mayor stood up, interrupted Darrell, and announced, "Everyone needs to know this." At an annual, state prayer breakfast, a tearful senator kneeled at Darrell's feet, imploring, "Tell us what to do." Darrell didn't have the formula he wanted but merely said, "You're doing it." Darrell knew policy born of genuine grief and compassion was the best hope for America. He knew that William Penn thought the same thing when he spoke of people's character being key to good policy.

Another senator, Stewart Greenleaf, carried around a bag of dirt in his pocket after reading our book, waiting for the day he could apologize to Native Americans. He humbled himself one day in front of our Mohawk friend, Willie, and ate the dirt. This same senator asked Darrell to write a resolution for the state to describe Penn's experiment in government. It took Darrell six months to

---

5   The phrase "good news" is commonly equated with the preaching of the gospel.

even think about doing it for reasons outside the scope of this writing. But when he finally wrote it, with the co-sponsorship of a dozen legislators, something was seriously going awry with Darrell.

Darrell was no longer the fun-loving sanguine man he once was. Besides being involved with the Penn story around the state and nation, Darrell had tried to reverse some difficulties our church had gone through in its past. We sincerely, but foolishly, absorbed too much of those costs, including using our security nest egg built up over our marriage. The exhortation from leaders in our denominational group was, "You can't outgive God" and "We all inherit problems when we take over churches." I once argued with a district supervisor, "Not ones with such immediate and personal consequences." Over time, these strains accumulated. I wanted to leave the state but neither of us could deny how our newly-formed relationships with lovely Pennsylvanians and the Penn story kept us believing in our purpose there.

Stress cracks began showing in our marriage. Darrell grew tired and increasingly distant over the last few years in Pennsylvania. We spoke frankly about it at first, even seeing a pastoral counselor. After hearing our story, our counselor believed we needed a three-month sabbatical. He warned of the consequences if we continued as we were, but the mechanism wasn't set up within our organization for a long absence. We asked for a sabbatical. The answer was that we needed to leave Pennsylvania. Instead of a break, we were sent home to Hawaii to canvas for the role of senior pastors at our home church.

A change would do it, so everyone hoped. Even us. When we traveled to Hawaii to explore the option of moving home, we spent time alone. I vividly remember how beautiful it felt to hold hands and rediscover us in familiar and safe stomping grounds. I liked him again! Our two lives zoomed together, and suddenly I knew it had been right to think of moving back home to Hawaii—for us. It seemed in the nick of time too. I felt a tremendous relief. However, hitting the ground running in a new role wasn't the proper solution. Warning signs increased and went unheeded. The opportunity to rest vanished. Ultimately, not taking a break exacted a toll that nearly destroyed our marriage. It certainly shattered Darrell's well-being. Even before these last years though, Darrell's physical health had been affected. At the time the first edition of the book was published in 2000, Darrell had sustained an inexplicable spinal cord injury to his neck. Then while writing the resolution in 2005, his heart developed a weird habit of stopping due to newly developed tachycardia. It sent him to the hospital on two occasions.

Finally, Darrell crashed emotionally and physically. When he was in Hawaii actively taking the lead role in our home church, the resolution he wrote, honoring William Penn as a Founding Father, hit the house floor at the Harrisburg Capitol for debate. After a fight between parties over the language, the Resolution passed remarkably word-for-word as Darrell wrote it. While the senator and his staff celebrated the rarity of a civilian writing a resolution to pass unanimously without changes, Darrell's doctor told him, "I don't know what you do for a living, but it's killing you." Not only was it killing him, it was killing our family. We no longer could reprove anyone for burnout as if they weren't up to the task.

Ultimately, we left church ministry and took that necessary sabbatical. But the process cost us many tangible securities, including our home, career, reputation, and finances. We couldn't fight it: Darrell was too broken. He had even lost his memory for a time as if he had a stroke. He probably did, according to one doctor's examination of him post-breakdown.

Friends had arranged for us to stay at a retreat center for leaders. At first, Darrell refused to go, scoffing, "What am I going to do for three months? And after that, what?" He was patterned to live in overdrive; he couldn't imagine life otherwise. After a month into it, he finally understood how exhausted and lost to himself he was. Once he gave himself entirely to the recovery process, he slept for days. When he was able to engage, we experienced a life-changing renaissance. One day we took a vineyard tour in the Shenandoah mountains, near our retreat center. We sat marveling along a creek with our bottle of wine and snacks. "How can we be completely absent from everything we were and yet be so completely content in the moment?" We dared not analyze it just in case we'd prick the happy bubble we were in. We were alive to every moment, not pushing off our happiness to the future anymore.

By June 2006, I was at least breathing in and out, convinced that we'd made it through the worst. We pushed our children too far by then anyway, especially our youngest who was a senior in high school. Our house in Pennsylvania sold just as our time was up in the mountains. We converged with our kids, moving to Virginia permanently. Darrell's memory was returning more and more every day, and it seemed like his health was better too. He never needed the surgery his cardiologist had recommended to sever a nerve in his heart.

Sometimes, I'd wake up to him looking at me, tears rolling down his face because he had been able to unwind a memory lost to him during his breakdown. As painful as some of that was for him to recall, it was restorative. I certainly hadn't forgotten the crazy, particularly the pain of his rejection of the children and me during the days when he was pushing away everything that had tethered him to life—his family, the church, and Penn. It was healing to revisit those difficult memories in the priceless context of brokenness and grace. It was necessary.

We were starting our lives over in critical ways, no longer having any past securities to rely on. So, when Darrell's birthday came around that year, I had to be creative with a gift. I wanted him to know I saw him and still believed in him, us, and our promises. I sat at the computer to write something for him. I felt every word. It was an allegory about our life, filled with hidden meanings and descriptions of our struggles, our faith, and our love. I rolled the one-page story into a scroll and tied it with a left-over ribbon. Without our usual birthday fanfare, I gave it to him while he sat on the edge of the bed, the one-room borrowed space we lived in. It went like this:

The Couple That Dared

Once upon a time, two young people dreamed of living in the Depths of Love and of slaying a great beast. And so, they set off… dreaming and daring along the way. They left the Easy Side of Love and entered uncharted lands. Passionate was their love and laughter along the way. Chiding weakness and warnings alike, they routed the enemies of both body and soul. Fear they knew not. They faced perils raw and rare. Bled they did, scarred they became. Wounded, they nurtured each other with the antidote only love knows… and beauty waned never. The deeper they traveled the more furious the fight. They continued in battle side by side, ever dreaming of traveling to the Depths of Love.

One day, a violent horde, sent by the master of the lesser dragons this couple had already slain, came to destroy this brave couple. So brutal the force this legion was, and so vast the territory to win, that they unhappily turned to fight separate fronts. Fighting alone and in the dark, they were desperate to unite again. They kept fighting these stronger foes, longing, remembering. They dreamed of being together and knew this great horde once defeated would no more keep them apart. But how long and how far could the strength, they once doubted not, go? Could these would-be fatal wounds heal if they not be united? Each had the other's antidote. Yet again and again their memory, their longing nursed them, kept them going. They feared for each other, no word of truth to hear. So lost they felt, so desperate for the sound of each other's voice.

After many moons in disenchanted places, one day a fierce wind blew exposing each member of the great horde. She longingly looked across the battlefield for her beloved, as she had hundreds of times before. But this final time he was there, beyond the horde, at the edge of the forest where it met the dry and rocky wilderness. He was so broken—so beaten—but alive and just as beautiful as the first time she saw him. She ran to his embrace, carried by the wind. He was as she remembered. Strength and passion blended once her gaze met his beautiful eyes. Drinking in the medicine of love and promise, they regained their passion and their peace.

At once the couple turned to see the evil horde tangled and driven off the land by the Great and Mighty Wind. "We made it," he said. "This battle is finally over." He slipped his hand into hers and led her into the trees, a new land where he said, "This is the place where one is the weapon, where two hands form one bow, where every battle is won with one sword, your hand in mine."

And they lived the rest of their lives in the Depths of Love. So profound, so evocative was the love of this couple that stories were written about them for those weak hearts who dared not, dreamed not, and chose not to leave the Easy Side of Love. For those who settled there could only dream. But this couple's love was like a magnificent masterpiece, where every hue and every value draws one to stare and imagine a thousand brave stories, while at the very same time tranquil, quiet, and full of light.

Darrell smiled gently as I gave him the scroll. He was always so grateful and sentimental about gifts. He kept cards and pictures drawn for him by our children. He even kept the pictures the children in our church drew when he was the pastor. I could tell he appreciated my effort. But as he unrolled the paper and began to read each line of my story, it was apparent that he was connecting to more than sentiment. He was reliving our marriage and our ministry, even as I had when I wrote it. I could see in his eyes that he knew exactly the hostility of specific battle fronts, as all the innocence and the zeal of our youth confronted the raw and unde-fended trauma in which we found our older selves.

His soul was working hard to reconcile his disillusionment with whatever promises remained despite it all. Tears flowed as the story viscerally touched our souls and seemed an open invitation into the pain. The private knowledge of hundreds of circumstances melted into one big celebration where a divine dance took place. More tears flowed and finally tight hugs and tender kisses.

There he was again: Darrell, the man I fell in love with on the beaches of Hawaii over twenty years previous. The pieces of our life that remained after our shakedown were our marriage, our family, and the story of William Penn. We started a nonprofit to continue telling the Penn story. These were by far the best years of our mar-riage, even though challenges emerged once we became active in our nonprofit. This time, however, none of those problems could separate us. Not once was Darrell depressed or disillusioned again. He couldn't be. He had disempowered his demons near and far, those inside him and those coming at him. This is not to say that he wasn't discouraged or grief-stricken at times, especially by the social ills for which he spent many hours in prayer. Out of grief which was no longer tied to his person, he could see and target his prayers more accurately.

Darrell fine-tuned his life message and reconceived what he saw as the limited language he used when writing *The Seed of a Nation*. He began writing again with deepening insights, still wor-ried that some public figures had misapplied and misunderstood Penn's principles. There was a need for more context. He felt he had inadvertently fueled a dangerous ideology of taking America back for God, some using the Penn story for confirmation. At times, folks sounded militant. One church leader argued with us, "We may have to take up arms to defend our rights." It was like they never read Penn at all.

In addition to all Darrell's upgrades, he gained an authentic message on gratitude. He lived in profound rest not dependent on circumstances, finances, or worldly accolades. His connection to God was inspiring, and his engagement with me was constant. Our intellectual and spiritual sparring was lifegiving as we re-imagined all the work yet to be accomplished.

Plenty of folks remarked how in love and engaged we were with each other, whether holding a historical tour, speaking together in public, or hanging with friends. We felt our harmony, but to know it showed made us celebrate how far we had come. Not all knew how we nearly lost each other. But now, when Darrell saw me, it was often like a reunion after a long absence; never mind, I might be just there in the next room. He rarely walked by me without touching me. He frequently queued music in my car's CD player to a love song he wanted me to hear. He was the best version of himself. Ever.

My birthday story was true as I lived it in the aftermath of a difficult season. Our two separate hands did join in one purpose, just as I had imagined. Our inner restoration was more valuable than our outward circumstances could boast. We owned less, had given all to ministry, had fewer cheerleaders, and yet, were happier than ever.

One day, we were at a restaurant with some peers, all catching up with each other. The stories were luxurious: new cars, adventurous travel, laurels awarded. We truly were happy and proud to hear all of it. Halfway through the stories, Darrell caught my eye across the table. I knew what he was feeling and thinking. We were in a different space right at that moment. He was asked what he's been up to. He merely said, "You know I heard this new song that reminded me of my wife. Would you like to hear it?" He pulled it up on his phone and played "Thinking Out Loud" by Ed Sheeran. He stared adoringly at me while the music played. Suddenly, there were no words left to speak to the room. Darrell didn't want to share that he was in conversations with legislators about writing a third resolution for the state of Pennsylvania. I wanted him to but understood why he didn't. It wasn't about his achievements, anymore. They were not even that extraordinary to him, just purposeful.

Darrell developed a life of unlimited, quiet joy. In that lasting state, he never became disillusioned again. "For who wants to live in an illusion," he'd say about the good coming to him from setbacks, from those few years of persistently scattering the shadows of his disappointment. We both knew that we were ready to take our story and our work to the next level. We were inspired and grateful to know that we were maturing in love and authenticity. It gave us confidence that we had been tested, proven, and were now equipped for what was next.

LIVING OUR
DREAM, ALMOST

arrell was magnificent at our first big fund-raising event for our nonprofit, The Seed of a Nation Gala, at the end of September 2018. His part of the program was to tell our history and how we had become so passionate about William Penn and his contributions to America and the world. Darrell was compelling—authentic, impassioned, and so incredibly handsome in his three-piece suit. There is nothing more attractive than a man who knows who he is and displays his gifts in humility and strength. That was Darrell that night. He smiled the entire time he spoke, as he always did during the past twenty-some years of public speaking in which I was not only his wife, but his parishioner as well as his partner.

I'd follow Darrell anywhere, even when following him brought so much trouble and pain. The gratitude and joy from our growth were nothing I imagined self-made humans could know. We were miraculously restored, refashioned, and transformed during our recent past, living in more peace than any self-help ever provided. We knowingly rejoiced that it took this long to get us right—to get the story right—for it was more than about William Penn. Besides, Penn hadn't gotten it all right either. It was about humanity reimagining itself in the context of love and intentional about love's requirements. We had to be true to ourselves if we were to authenticate our message. That is why Darrell was so believable that night... why anyone is believable. Only when we know our growth is entwined with humanity's can we impact anything or anyone. It's arrogant and demeaning to think we bring all the answers to the people. We now saw ourselves as part of a continuum: the unfinished business of civilization to live in harmony with God, nature, and each other.

Darrell was all that personified. We believed we were ready only after decades of learning and placing ourselves in the context correctly, or at least better than we had ever imagined. We were ready to invite the world to join us. That was the point of our gala. Darrell did something odd that night as he introduced me. He told the audience that it was no longer about him. He said it was all about me and what I was accomplishing. He knew that I had taken the story further than he could have and now supported my lead.

In a male-dominated world, it was easy for folks to place him in the lead role. I could see that he wanted to set me up to succeed and take attention off of him even although he had started this whole thing.

The first book would have looked entirely different without me; but for a long time, that was a little secret. He had been completely humbled and repentant that he had ever draped himself in his accomplishments, not that they weren't newsworthy. They were. He just knew that his ego was in the mix. If he were here now, he'd say it straight up. He spoke many times to others about his transformation. His elevation of me that night was not only because of his personal growth, but it was necessary for the story to be told for the larger picture of equality and inclusion.

In a male-dominated world, it was easy for folks to place him in the lead role. I could see that he wanted to set me up to succeed and take attention off of him even though he had started this whole thing. Darrell was the one who wrote state resolutions and attracted so much attention to the story. But now, it would be my skills and education about the historical context telling the story we wanted the world to embrace. However true we knew my role would be, I didn't want him to say it so absolutely. I needed him and the authority he gained in his years of sacrifice and service. I needed his passion because it was like no other. I was a bit disquieted that he took this giant step back, pushing me to the forefront. Some of our board of advisors and friends had also commented on this. I knew they would.

We received glowing reviews for the gala, some telling us we changed their minds about fund-raisers. The food, the music, the people, he and I, were great. We were set. We had multiple projects to fund and reason to believe the Seed's income would increase. We'd finally be producing our new material. My history degree and screenwriting education would all pay off. I was super energized and inspired.

Nonetheless, my world immediately began to crumble after the gala, eventually wiping away any remnants of the high I had enjoyed. I had to fly to Los Angeles for The American Film Market the day after the gala. I also needed to see my sister, who was in her final stages of breast cancer. I was still in California two weeks after the gala when Darrell collapsed in pain. He assumed that it was food poisoning after his agony subsided. I made him promise to go to the emergency room if it happened again.

I returned from the West to our home in the Shenandoah Mountains, where I had secluded myself to write. It was November now—the crisp air and the changing leaves inspired me. I put some touches on my mapped-out television series and continued working on a hundred-year timeline as a tool for writers who would eventually come onto the project. I sent my pilot episode to one of my instructors for a critique. I was having so much fun!

Stunned. I stood looking out my writing window at the brilliant fall scene now betraying my world.

A few days later Darrell traveled to Virginia Beach to take care of some things and see our children, all of whom lived in the city. He filled in the gaps of our absence by staying connected to our family while I worked hard to finish and package our material for marketing to production companies. I was busily working when I received word from my brother, informing me my sister had died. I had just begun to feel the impact of that terrible news when Darrell called. He rambled on about being in pain again, every detail: his inability to move, what position he lay in, when he could get up, and on and on.

"So?" I interrupted. I needed the punchline first.

He continued, "Well, I finally got up and made the bed..."

Blah, Blah, Blah. I could just see him—in pain—making the bed. "And you folded your nightclothes exactly as you have done for thirty-four years. Darrell, WHAT?" I impatiently demanded.

"I drove to Wawa to get a mocha and then went to the emergency room," he persisted, now being ridiculous.

"This isn't funny, Darrell," I chided.

Then, it was silent... for a long few seconds. I began to tremble instinctively. "Hon, they say I have kidney cancer," he gently spilled out.

Stunned. I stood looking out my writing window at the brilliant fall scene now betraying my world. I snapped out of it and rushed to my friends next door to tell them I was leaving for who knows how long. They, Irv and Kathy, cried with me and wrapped me in the biggest hug. I ran back to my villa to pack. I was befuddled. I brought random clothing items and managed to pack my books, my printed scripts, some research, and my computer. On the way down the mountain, which I have traveled many dozens of times, I forgot to take an exit and ended up going fifty miles out of my way, a one-hundred-mile detour. I didn't even recognize where I was. I was talking to a trusted friend when a sign alerted me, "Oh. My. God. Debbie, I am part way to Pennsylvania on the 81!" Instead of taking four-ish hours, it took me five and a half to get to Virginia Beach. I was wrecked.

I arrived at Darrell's hospital room. There was a commotion booming from inside. When I opened the door I witnessed Darrell, my children, and my friends (Bill and Nancy) all seemingly having a party of sorts, snacks and all. Their laughter cluttered my grisly reality. I stood there with quizzical eyes and assessed. Darrell saw me and immediately called me to his bedside. He grabbed me knowingly with the comfort only he could give.

Darrell was full of joy, optimism, and love. He told me of an eleven-centimeter growth that needed to be removed but related that there was no rush. "Apparently kidney cancer grows slowly according to the doctor," Bill added. Wait, what? I needed more. But Bill, our children, and Darrell moved on to the topic at hand before I came along: the quirks of the doctor. They roared hysterically retelling me one story after the next. Yet, my mind wandered.

Their stories faded into the background. What's the nature of renal carcinoma? "Apparently" was a word that didn't comfort me. How did anyone know how fast it was growing? I immediately implored Google and visited the National Institute of Health's website from my phone. Darrell noticed, "Hon, it's gonna be fine," he whispered and nudged me back to the ecosystem of the room. I took a look around the happy space. Truly, it was normal for us to be hopeful.

My beautiful family and friends were so full of courage, love, and laughter. I took a deep breath. I was grateful. I needed them just as they were to recover from my traumatic drive where my mind went wild with speculation. We were just fine. In that very moment, we were perfectly us. Soon, the doctor returned. I chuckled perceptively when he began with the same antics earlier described by my comedic family. They were correct: the doctor was eccentric. He unwittingly became material for this creative group, some of which were, and still are, predisposed to write stand-up comedy. This was on November 13, 2018, just shy of three weeks before my 57th birthday.

The Thanksgiving holiday jeopardized Darrell's fight with cancer. Our team of surgeons took their leisure to return from their vacations to join our urgent plight. While Darrell appeared to have little concern during this time, I was the kildeer mother bird, frantically flapping my wings while screaming to draw the monster away from my loved one. By the time Darrell was wheeled into the operating room twenty-tree days after his diagnosis, I had amassed tons of research and knowledge of clinical trials. I could identify standards of treatment. I met with nutritionists and began a radical diet for Darrell, creating concoctions that my dear man placated me to swallow. His eyes lovingly comforted me as he dutifully ingested my homemade remedies. Never had a blender served me better.

> The doctor and I exchanged a knowing smile about this man who refused the gravity of what was about to happen.

December 6, 2018, arrived. On the way to the hospital, Darrell unleashed his vocal cords to fill the car with ballads to Heaven. After being admitted, Darrell was carted to a makeshift overflow area where patients awaited their surgeries. I followed. It was dreary. We heard nothing but moans and monitors in this assembly line of sick humans, but Darrell wouldn't have it be bleak on his big day. He translated the room with a classic hymn. He sang, elongating the notes of "Great is Thy Faithfulness" as if he were trying out for Pavarotti. The lead surgeon walked in on his performance with a quizzical smile that said, "This is not normal." Darrell stopped mid-verse and called the surgeon to his side like he had a plan. He did. The pre-op meeting was now a photo-op and Darrell was the director. I obliged and took pictures of them in their surgical caps and gowns. The doctor and I exchanged a knowing smile about this man who refused the gravity of what was about to happen. His levity helped me gather for myself all the positive faith and energy he had. If anybody could make it through with sheer optimism, it was he.

Eight hours ticked by slowly as my children and I waited. Surgery took longer than expected. We calmed ourselves with stories of Darrell. I idiotically tried to review some of my work. Somehow, in my mind, it was hard to believe this was all real. Darrell's sudden collapse was deja vu in a way. While I can't prove correlation in any of this, it felt like the time Darrell had sustained that unexplainable spinal cord injury when the book was published... and then had that breakdown on the day the resolution he wrote for the state of Pennsylvania passed. There were other strange coincidences like this too. This new attack on his person and body was coincidentally timed with our gala event and the rejuvenation we were experiencing in our latest work. I needed to believe this cancer wasn't real or wasn't going to be.

Furthermore, Darrell had so much more to do before he left this world. His insights in the last few years were so profound that I sometimes trembled at their implications. Often I would begin recording him as he downloaded critical nuances the message *The Seed of a Nation* needed. There had been growing louder a wing of Christianity focused on wanting to use American history as a mandate to colonize power within politics for a religious vision. He felt that was opposite of the Gospel testimony. He wanted to fix his part in that, amending his language and theology since it had been upgraded during his sabbatical reflections and beyond.

If he were here now he would speak to the division and chaos in our nation and be positive that it just might be useful as raw material to reorient the world to a new vision for peace. He would be attaching his faith to that effect since an overreaction to injustice merely creates more injustice and skews original issues. It was incredible to us that a gospel in which some of the most famous teachings, like loving your enemies, had been so lost on so many throughout history and up until today.

A call to love is disruptive in its purest form because it disallows everything that is *not* love. We figured that bit out the hard way.

I know Darrell (and Penn) would have been appalled to see and hear those who violently stormed the Capitol on January 6th breakout in prayer in the Senate chamber, thanking God for favor. Yet, Darrell would also be content that it so blatantly revealed the mindset we were trying to expose through storytelling, since saying it straight up all those years wasn't as easy as we had imagined. A call to love is disruptive in its purest form because it disallows everything that is *not* love. We figured that bit out the hard way.

Darrell's role felt even more critical to me now than ever. I imagined he and William Penn being able to speak in unison about the habitual use of conflict and war to justify perceived *noble* worldviews. Penn summed up this default—this global behavior—and basically said, "Now that we know what doesn't work, (my para-phrase) *let us* [finally] *try what love will do.*"[6]

The Seed of a Nation Gala was Darrell's coming out of this season of reflection and devoted intercession. So, in my mind, this illness couldn't take him out of this world. Darrell had come to know this Penn story wasn't about Penn after all, even though Penn remained his hero. It's just that he wasn't going to be as sympathetic about Penn in a way that sounded hegemonic, skirted the truth, or avoided his failures. The story was the indirect way to get to moti-vations that prevented peace, particularly those that misrepresented God to populations of people. He was completely sober about the next phase of our lives. It was sober because mindsets don't change easily, and when he had faced those collective beliefs in the past, the backlash was brutal, especially because the ferocity of some of those who claimed to be followers of Christ could be blatant.

If anyone could love his way into the hearts of people while speaking the hard stuff, it was Darrell. He wasn't prepared before— but now he was. He and I developed an appreciation for our strug-gles, knowing that we had to be transformed and matured to authenticate this nuanced version of Penn, the gospel, and societal peace. And we knew there were a lot of peaceful people looking for another way, confused about politics and religion, who could attach their faith to such a story in a way to excite the imagination for the future.

To me, this illness was a ruse. Darrell had a job here on planet Earth, and that was that. Besides, it would be inconceivable that I could carry the load alone. I needed him for my part in that

---

6   William Penn, *Some Fruits of Solitude.* (New York and Boston H.M. Caldwell Co.,1903) [Pdf] Library of Congress, https://loc.gov/item/03020370/.

task, too. It was my birthday allegory about our mutual passion all over again. This next effort was going to be—had to be—us at our true best, strengthened by our experiences and by our marital love, which was more passionate than ever. We weren't afraid anymore.

Eight and a half hours now ticked by before the doctor finally found me, my children, and some friends, chatting in a corner of the waiting room. She looked exhausted. She sat and folded her hands in her lap. I watched as if she were in slow motion. She told us that the team of surgeons had removed Darrell's kidney and a football-sized tumor. We learned that along with Darrell's left kidney, he no longer had his spleen and a portion of his stomach. The fast-growing monster had also been stuck to his intestines. She told us that she gotten all she could. We'd have to wait for pathology to know for sure. I was flabbergasted.

Darrell returned to his hospital room with a diagonal two-foot incision across his torso and a spinal drip of Fentanyl. He again transformed his room into a celebration gathering almost immediately after he woke. He was his goofy, grateful, happy self for the next ten days of his hospital recovery. Often friends would come to offer comfort yet leave being comforted by him. His energy was on overdrive; there was no room for fear or doubt. He was cute, too, like a boy bragging about his scars and victories won, and innocent like a young man showing off his biceps to his father.

We went home and waited for the pathology report for another week. When we walked into the urologist's office for the report, a strange quiet settled over the staff behind the counter. All of them, and I mean ALL of them, watched us walk by. Suddenly, a shudder ran down my spine. Every step to the patient room was a felt act. They knew something we didn't. Our doctor smiled at us in the exam room. She humored Darrell's casual comment and then got to the business at hand. She read the grimmest of words and spoke of the pathologist's questioning her about what kind of cancer this was supposed to be, indicating the rarity of Darrell's illness. I felt the anxiety rush through my body. I just needed her to get to the end. When she did, she said, "We couldn't get clear margins."

I already knew what that meant from my surplus of research. It meant that nasty cancer was still recruiting Darrell's good cells and was still active. She instructed us to see her recommended oncologist. I canceled our appointment with the first oncologist, that funny man who said kidney cancer grows slowly. He was wrong, and nothing was funny about that.

We descended from this meeting through the staff area once more. It felt like we were in the movie *The Quiet Place*. One misstep and we'd be discovered and eaten alive. We tiptoed in silence to our car, eyes piercing our backs. We were stunned by the news, but not exactly able to trust the doctor's bleak words. I had read of a case where a man had stage four sarcomatoid renal cancer and was now cancer-free. That was going to be Darrell. I would do all I could to make sure. But those eyes said even more than the doctor and frightened me. Darrell saw that my heart showed on my face, "This is not our only reality or truth, hon." Darrell smiled long at me from the passenger seat until I could return one to him. Then, I drove us off into the unknown from that pathology reading.

HE LEADS US
TO HIS DEATH

I t was Christmas immediately after we received the grim pathology report, but Darrell was determined that it would be our best. He spent money we couldn't spare like it was his last Christmas; he even hinted as much when I questioned his spending. I couldn't accept that reality. Had I been able to believe he wouldn't be with us much longer, I would *not* have sabotaged our traditional Christmas breakfast by making everyone eat almond flour biscuits (my attempt to starve the cancer of carbs) rather than the fluffy buttermilk ones we eagerly awaited all year. My gracious family ate the hockey puck-like fritters, not improved one bit by drowning them in our annual sausage gravy. Nonetheless, they had nothing but smiles, gratitude, and attempted compliments on the biscuits. Their barely veiled effort to be gracious made us all laugh.

Christmas day continued gingerly. Our children were absorbing the news that their dad still had cancer growing in him after surgery. That detail might not have seemed so real had it not been obvious by now Darrell was fighting for his life. He was barely hiding his increasing pain. He was thin, rapidly losing weight now but not like the usual kind of weight loss. His muscles were being harvested for the energy needed by the monster inside him. I felt

like I was staring down the devil behind the curtain of my husband's body. I hated that thing.

My prayers then and in the following months were fierce, cursing the evil, commanding Darrell's body to do its job and not be tricked by rogue cells that seduced the healthy ones to its cause by brazenly sending out sweet-tasting tendrils as a ploy to avoid prowling t-cells. I thought I had the power to speak to it as if cancer were an entity. I thought my love and faith would be strong enough. I thought I knew cancer's strategies. Besides, I had seen plenty of miracles before like when my lupus had been healed and when Darrell had regained feeling in his body after his spinal cord injury. There was more… like Jeffrey graduating high school when his neurologist said he'd be severely diminished after the auto accident… like when our marriage was lifted to the stratosphere after Darrell's catastrophic emotional and physical crash when I thought all could be lost… like all the stories our family shared seeing breakthrough after breakthrough in each life and when the impossible turned possible… like when one of us, once blinded to reality, could suddenly see clearly… like when, in our individual and communal lives, we so often traded weakness for strength in the middle of challenges. If ever we needed these kinds of renewals, it was now.

In January, we saw a top-rated oncologist, who gave us hope. I handed him my research on a course of treatment for a man I read about who had recovered from stage four renal cancer. He had a more aggressive medicine to try first. It was a fifty-thousand-dollar expense each month. We waited three weeks for this poison to be specially delivered with its skull and crossbones warning all over the packaging. In the meantime, a new pain immobilized Darrell. He had more tests and more MRIs, but no one could figure it out.

Darrell couldn't stand up without excruciating pain radiating from high up under his rib cage and into his left shoulder.

I researched what nerves would be affected in the area of Darrell's pain and realized that they were in the neck. I suggested he see a chiropractor. However, the chiropractor would not touch him after he saw a mass in Darrell's neck from the X-rays he took. We immediately contacted our oncologist, who ordered a new round of tests. We saw a neurosurgeon who confirmed that cancer was now in Darrell's cervical spine.

February and March were a blur. We were in a fast-paced montage. Darrell's pain was excruciating even on morphine, but he was heroic and really good at living in the moment. When friends came from out of town to visit him, he would say "We're not going to focus on me; let's be as we always have been." Once we set Darrell up at the end of the bed so he could recline, pushed a card table up close, and played Rummy Cube for hours. That night, Darrell was in extra pain from the festivities, but all he said was how much fun he had. This happened on repeat as he laughed, prayed, and sang with everyone that came. I was proud of his generosity and how he could connect to each person. After Darrell's brothers, Steve and Jeff, returned to their homes, Darrell related to me in tears, grasping his heart, "Did you see in their eyes how much love they had?" He was so blessed but also hurt for them that they had to see him sick. He felt the same about all our friends who came. But I was particularly awestruck by the exchange he had with his men buds: bravado abandoned to the soulful truth of love. I saw it clearly when our friend Dan (and his wife Vicki) came. It was like I was getting to peek into a part of masculinity that perhaps the world has dampened except in fox holes and tragedy. Every man may need a dangerous adventure and a problem to solve. But every person needs to know a love stronger than death, even men. I saw it. The willingness to be exposed is not weak. It's power. I loved these men loving each other like that. It made the air thick, like a balm of healing could be had.

Not all of it was as easy as Darrell was trying to make it seem, though. He was humiliated by how his body was breaking down and how others saw him. Once he even said to me for my apparent troubled expression, "Stop looking at me like I am dead already." One day in early February, he looked hard at himself in the mirror after his shower. His skin, once tight against his muscular build, was starting to hang.

He said to me, "I look like s—t. Darrell rarely used a curse word, but sometimes there's not anything better to use. This was one of those times; besides, it was true. He was emaciated, not at all the hunk of a man he had always been and was only a few months before. That wasn't the worst of it. He was in pain. He suffered. He was being eaten alive, and it was unbearable at times. When we were alone, his moans of pain were gut-wrenching, yet he consistently found respite in his music. One day I asked how he could remain engaged with people, with me, and with God while in so much pain. He replied to me in terms of sacrifice. I recorded it in February 2019.

> I do want to say there is a depth of worship that is involuntary when suffering has its way. It's like something deep within one's spirit evolves out of worship, out of love for God. It comes from suffering. The only thing that makes sense comes from your spirit man because the physical man is wrecked. Being able to

worship God… it's the only thing that is left. I don't know if I can put it into words, honey.

After a long pause, a glance, and a small upturning of his lips, Darrell muses again.

> It's the only thing that makes sense, bypassing everything natural. It becomes so deep and supernatural. It's spiritual. It lifts you to a new place. It gives you freedom. Suffering brings sacrifice because, in the end, it is the only thing that is real. You know it's real because the pain would want you to stop but there's a genuine sacrifice that is willing to suffer to make it to that place. It's very real, and genuine. You know? I've come to this new place. I love this place. It's very real. It's just happening. You cannot manufacture it. It's born in you.
>
> I am not sad. I am not remorseful. I am not regretful. I am overjoyed. I feel so close to God. If heaven can be here, it is here… right now. It feels so close. He is here. He's very much here. It's real, honey. He's very tangible.

There were other heart-wrenching moments when he regretted the possibility of missing out on our children's and grandchildren's lives. The day he pondered what our newly born grandson, Luca, would be like. It pierced my soul, not only for his loss but for Luca's. Luca's little life would be immeasurably enriched if Darrell lived. "Do you think he will be creative like his dad, his mom… like you? Will he like sports, music, or both? Will he be rough and tumbly? Will he be funny and quirky?" I knew where he was going with that last bit, "You mean like you?" I asked. He smiled.

There were plenty of tough conversations with our children, like when Brian sat at the edge of Darrell's bed questioning, "If God can do anything… then why?" He tells us how difficult it was to lose it in front of his daughter Evangeline, who, as a five-year-old, tried to comfort him. He didn't know how to explain it to her. Or, when Sarah grieved for not having had children by saying Brian would get to see Darrell through his two children but she would "not have him [Darrell] anymore." Or, when Jeffrey wondered how he could survive without Darrell, who was his safety net. Jeffrey cried one day remembering how Darrell instinctively reached to steady him stepping off a ladder or walking on precarious surfaces. He remembered the time Darrell had rescued him from flipping his kayak. All these and more Darrell provided without a word of exposure about Jeffrey's brain injury and its lasting consequence on Jeffrey's equilibrium.

One particular day Darrell wept uncontrollably after he asked me to read to him Sarah's Facebook post about his cancer. He said he didn't want to die because she (and the boys) needed him.

"There's just too much to lose if I pass away, he said. "I want to love Sarah every day. I want to see her every day. She brings me so much joy. I feel like I lost sight of her for a time. I see her. I see her all over again. She's precious. She's beautiful. She's a creation."

He paused grimacing, "This pain is stealing my life," he moaned, shifting his body.

"Please show me her post again." I showed him the post, it included before and after photos, and then I read:

I have no words. I am grieving. I am happy, I am broken, and I am strong. Papa Bear, summer 2018, Montana and Warm Springs versus winter 2019 in Cancerville. I am at the place where you want to cuddle with your parents like you are five again. I am very close to my parents. And this is hard! Life is glorious but so much beyond what I am prepared for. Maranatha. I hate cancer!

Darrell began a new treatment. The neurosurgeon wouldn't touch the cancer in Darrell's neck in an operation; it was too dangerous, he said. The next best thing was targeted radiation to stop the cancer from entering his spinal column. Darrell thought the technology of the machine was cool because it looked like an AT-ST from *Star Wars*. Of course, Darrell again, had me taking celebratory pictures of this process to which the technicians had to make accommodations for my being in the room. I once told him, "You know this isn't as fun as you think?" But he wouldn't be deterred.

I was waiting for him to finish a session of radiation one day when Darrell walked around the corner and proclaimed, with hands raised high to a gray room full of very sick patients and their worn family members. "Victory!" I first thought about the poor folks being forced to compare their experience with his. The radiation, however, left Darrell with a detached scapula but gave him several pain-free weeks. He began to walk in the neighborhood. It was the best he had felt since November. Yet, it wasn't to last.

Simultaneously, the chemo drug was destroying Darrell's immune system. He developed horrible sores in his mouth and could hardly eat or drink. Our oncologist started Darrell on a new medication after attending a conference and learning of a new treatment plan for rare cancers. It was, coincidentally, the exact treatment plan I gave him from my research on the first day we met him. But now Darrell's cancer load was so much greater. The new MRI showed his belly filled with tumors. It was a thick, invading forest destroying his stomach and other organs. All I could think was, it's too late now. My head spun with regrets. Had we missed the only opportunity to kill this cancer when it was at its weakest right after surgery? It was torture that even my best efforts weren't enough, and my advocacy for Darrell seemingly went unheard.

We returned for a follow-up visit with his surgeon in March 2019. I pressed her on the oncologist's plan. For the first time, I considered the possibility that Darrell wasn't being treated for a cure after all. I dare not say it out loud, but when Darrell questioned her about a prognosis, she said, "Darrell, this is what is going to take you from this world. We just don't know if that's this year or in five years." We never had a prognosis to this point. This was our first. It was pure grief to hear.

Darrell ended up in the hospital several more times. The first time was after he fell when the blunt force of his body hitting the ground (he wasn't strong enough to stop the fall with his arms) caused swelling in his belly. At least, that was what we thought at first. It turned out fluids were building up in his body as one of cancer's cascading consequences. The plan was to drain it to relieve the swelling in his belly. By now, I knew what that meant from my late-night readings through medical journals, but I said nothing to Darrell. He was losing albumin, which keeps fluid within the cardiovascular system when in supply. Now his veins were leaking. This was the beginning of the end, according to the research. Without a miracle, which I was still directing my faith towards, he didn't have long to live.

Darrell continued to display confidence. A friend showed up one day while we were in the hospital. He and Darrell engaged in dialogue about hospitality, of all things. He shared thoughts that were insightful to me. First, he emphasized, "It's not just about serving or offering accommodations to people but rather hospitality was about receiving people, bringing them into your life, just as they are, and showing them love and acceptance. It's welcoming them free of judgments. We offer this to people, this generous free space to just be, this is hospitality." Darrell concluded by saying that hospitality, kindness, and generosity were, in his view, three key elements of authentic faith. Our friend, who came to encourage us left with a message he said he was going to speak that day at the university where he worked.

While in the hospital at the end of March, the palliative care team visited us. Darrell had rejected their visits twice now. That day we listened. The hard reality was they needed to speak to us about Darrell's prognosis, which was clearer now than when his surgeon had told us this disease would take Darrell's life, a subject our oncologist never broached. They used words like eminent, hospice, and death. They told us clearly that our oncologist was not treating Darrell for a cure but only to extend his life. That was what I increasingly feared but didn't want to hear, as if by doing so the speeding train called death would come into view.

It was decided we must speak in these terms to our children, saying it wouldn't be fair not to give them a chance to process part of their grief while Darrell was still here. The palliative care team would come back the next day. This would be hard. We asked our pastoral friend, Joseph, to come as support, not knowing how our family would react.

Darrell's hospital room was large, with a sofa and dining table. Our children and five-month-old grandson arrived, all seemingly their cheerful selves. They bantered with their dad and related their adventures. When the doctor and nurse walked in, it all changed. Their smiles were wiped clean off their faces. They quickly found their seats as if scripted. They listened. They teared up. They cried. The word "eminent" was shooting daggers in their hearts.

Death was just around the corner, so they told us. The starkness of it was in harsh relief. It's not that we never considered it; we hoped and believed we could cheat it. The conversation steered to the next steps. Darrell said he wanted to return home one last time (we hadn't been since his diagnosis). However, before he finished his sentence, Sarah blurted out, "So you're just going to die in the mountains?" Our boys began swallowing hard as Sarah summed up the moment. Before addressing our frantic daughter, Darrell excused the palliative care team saying, "We've heard and understood, but now I need time alone with my family."

Immediately as the door shut, Darrell gathered our children's attention. His first words were, "We are not going to make this about death. Come on guys, we are going to make this about life." He went on to tell them how much he had enjoyed life, loved it with them, and loved all his adventures and opportunities. He told them how he loved and learned from his struggles even more than his victories. He said they shouldn't take their failures to themselves any more than they should take their victories to themselves. He told them it was their time to love life to its fullest. He exhorted them to live.

> He finally told them out of everything he could give them, there was one thing he wanted to leave them most: joy.

The atmosphere of the room shifted from fear to love. He finally told them out of everything he could give them, there was one thing he wanted to leave them most: joy. He deliberately looked into all our faces. "I leave you joy," he said smiling, eyes brimming with tears.

One by one, our children, beginning with our son-in-law, Chase, told Darrell how much he meant to them. The tears were hot streaming down my cheeks as I listened to beautiful sentiments freely pouring from our children's hearts. I realized how privileged we were as a family to share these words of life while we were all still breathing in the land of the living. I watched my husband lead these children through their toughest season of life—losing him. He smiled the whole time he spoke. Darrell had grown to be their confidant, their friend, and their support system. Some people are forced to grieve over what could never have been; but our kids would suffer for the having, for being denied what was theirs.

On the one hand, it made them so grateful; on the other hand, it crudely cut a vital part of them off. Our friend, Joseph, could hardly interject when Darrell asked if he had anything to add. He summed up his comments by acknowledging the miracle he just witnessed. It was... and truly powerful. Darrell vanquished fear from that room, not just for himself but for us all. His leadership and confidence blew my mind. This was at the end of March 2019. We returned to our friends' house when Darrell was released from the hospital, where the next month was lived as if it was lifted from the calendar—it was its private complete world, our limited eschatological timeline. Feelings of foretelling bleakness punctuated every second of every day. I tried to fight it and stay positive for him, but it finally felt eminent. It was like the edge of Niagara Falls was just there as we floated helplessly toward it, the roar becoming louder and louder. My prayers were uttered fiercely with the reality that he would die. That thought fueled my prayers like never before.

One day Darrell could get out of the bath alone. The next I had to lift him. One day he could get down the stairs. The next not. I was persistently trying to feed him. I asked one time, "Aren't you ever hungry dear?" "No, I am not but I don't want to disappoint you," he replied with pleading eyes. It broke my heart that he tried to accommodate me when in reality, cancer had reduced his stomach to a slit, barely distinguishable on the MRI. I backed off, not wanting to torment my husband with my need to *do something*. I felt more helpless than ever and more relinquished to the fact that he may be gone soon. Yet, even with that thought, I wanted to believe that he could be healed and come back to me. I fantasized about that miracle. I didn't like to think I was bargaining with God, but perhaps I was dangling a proposition that he might want to get earthly credit for this rare event. I felt as foolish as I might have by handing a wealthy man cash for a gift.

My imagination housed the change in my mind, morphing from Darrell's being healed on this side of death to his being healed after. Darrell could go to Heaven and then come back, I reasoned.

We knew stories of near-death experiences, so I didn't think I was being seduced into magical thinking. I might have been. I didn't care. We made a pact. It went like this: once Darrell had died, he would hang out in this unearthly space and then ask to return. I'd be waiting with his body. When he returned he'd be suddenly healed. Tada! Darrell appeased me, half-jokingly, saying he would ask for a heavenly passport to come back to me.

Less than three weeks before Darrell died, he was reclining in a chair listening to the song "I Can Only Imagine" with tears streaming down his face. I asked, "Are you afraid?" He looked long at me, examined me, and searched to know my mood. He merely shook his head no, but said something interesting. He admitted he was vexed about one thing. "What will I do when I get there?" he asked. I answered him that I didn't think that would be a concern. "I imagine you will be living in everlasting peace and joy and there will be no more pain," I said as I began to cry.

Silence ensued as we sat together. Darrell studied me. A few minutes later he asked what I was thinking. I said, "I am thinking I am going to miss you." He pulled me to him with his weak grip. "Come here," he implored. I was careful not to touch his torso. His pain was great. Cheek to cheek, I sobbed as I hovered over him. The reality that would soon be mine wrapped tightly around my soul. It felt suffocating.

We were staying at Bill and Nancy's. When the surgeon told us this cancer was what would take Darrell from this planet, I started looking for temporary housing since it was impossible to go back home because of Darrell's treatments. We had been staying with Bill and Nancy since the diagnosis, but I began to consider the big ask it could be if Darrell died in their home. Ironically Nancy had been diagnosed with breast cancer nearly at the same time as Darrell had been diagnosed with kidney cancer. She was well on her way to total health by then, so she no longer needed my help. Sometimes, when Bill had to work I'd be at the house running up and down the stairs to see to Darrell's and her needs. It was crazy, but we shared a camaraderie that comforted us amid the trial we all were in. After thirty years of friendship, we completely had each other's trust.

"What if he dies... here? I cannot... will not ask that of you."

When Bill and Nancy got wind I was looking for housing, they held a little meeting with me standing around their kitchen island. They told me it was no time to set up a house elsewhere. I implored in tears, "But what if Darrell doesn't recover?" I didn't want to say the next words but I had to be clear. "What if he dies... here? I cannot... will not ask that of you." They looked me squarely in the eyes, "If he dies, it will be our great honor for you two to be in our home," Bill said while Nancy held my hand. I gasped. That sentence defined our radical friendship and their radical expression of love. Their confession nearly dropped me to my knees. We cried together and said no more.

April 7, 2019, was Jeffrey's birthday. We had a tradition of celebrating big on birthdays, and this was no different. Our children, Jeffrey, Brian, our daughter-in-law, Margarita, Sarah, our son-in-law, Chase, and Jeffrey's girlfriend, Melody, and her father, were all coming for dinner. I was happy about the excursion away from my worry. Everything was set. All I had to do was get Darrell downstairs. When I went to get him, with the aid of Jeffrey, Darrell begged for a pardon, "Please, I can't." You all have a good time. I will listen from here." He apologized to Jeffrey, "I am sorry, son." We knew what he was feeling in that moment, aware of the humiliation of his body betraying him. The struggle getting up and down the stairs came with moans, labored breathing, near falls, and my need to steady and lift him to every next step.

Instead, Jeffrey and I rushed to the kitchen and announced that the party would be upstairs. It wasn't that unusual, anyway. We had plenty of bedroom picnics over the last months with the family scattered around the room. Everyone helped by hauling the party up to Darrell. Our children were as they always had been, full of life and personal stories that kept everyone entertained and laughing. Darrell was having a blast in his recliner, his feet propped by pillows even further than the chair could lift them; it was necessary due to that menacing, vein-leaking problem. Darrell enjoyed the biggest meal I had seen him eat in days. The commotion was life-giving to him. Our six-year-old granddaughter, Evangeline, in true form, directed the room the best she could by ramping up her volume to organize a game, changing the rules to suit her, and giving us all so much delight.

When everyone left, Darrell marveled with me about the wonder of these humans we were privileged to call ours. His reflections inspired me. I told him to wait. I retrieved my computer and began to type. I transcribed Darrell's thoughts that night:

> The beauty of their laughter, the beauty of their joy; they emanate such joy when they are together. The beauty that comes out of their mouths is so rapturous; it's just a wondrous sound to hear. It's so beautiful. And it emanates from everywhere. Nobody is exclu-

sive. It's the most beautiful thing. It's contagious, you know. You can just lay here, Lorrie, and listen. You'll hear echoes of love, yes, but it's a sound of connectivity, coming from Jeffrey, Margarita, Brian, Chase, Sarah— all at the same time and, yet, it seems perfectly scored, no confusion in it; there was absolutely no confusion in it whatsoever.

It was like falling from the sky. If I were to say any-thing to them about the future, I would tell them to make the effort to be together, always. Oh, yes, make the effort. And just wait and see what comes out… because I think it will even surprise them… and it will lift their spirits and take them to places they need to go. Do you know why they need to go there? Because it changes them, transforms and makes them into better human beings. Yes, it does.

That love, that connectivity, they need to experi-ence it. Yes, they love each other. They know that, but it's not enough. They have to put in the time! Yes, yes… put int the time. So beautiful! You know and their laughter is genuine. Do you know that? They really feel it for each other. It's not selfish. They have experiences caused by the other person: [Chuckle] beautiful, hard, passionate, painful, sad, happy. All of those received from each other because of love.

They love you so much, Lorrie. They love you so much. Yeah, they do. But you're gonna find an unin-hibited love coming from them to you. It's gonna knock your socks off. I just know.

Brian: I enjoy Brian's freedom. I love his freedom. He's so free. He's like a butterfly, flitting about. [Chuckle] Just that expression, to discover somebody who can be so free and uninhibited. To clown around. He has inexpressible joy. He just loves to laugh. [chuckle] Do you hear that? Do you make sense of that? Broke my heart when troubled times took that from him. But, he's back. He is both strength and sensitivity. Not many people can carry both smartly. Others may try to take that from him again. But, he will handle it. He's back. He's back. I love him so much. He's my boy.

Jeffrey: I enjoy Jeffrey's freedom too. Jeffrey. He just rolls his head back and he doesn't care who thinks what. He just lets it roll. [chuckle] Jeffrey knows what freedom is, he knows what laughter is. He's the same but in a different way than Brian. I love how he always comes back to say goodbye. That's what Jeff does. "Is there anything I can do to help you, Dad? What can I do for you, Dad?" That's Jeff, thinking of others first. Jeffrey! You bet he is a good boy all the way through. He's so compassionate. And funny [chuckles]. He sure is. Witty, very witty. [chuckles] He's a witty kid.

Sarah: Wow. She is a bouquet of roses, no not roses. It's more than that. She has a different treasure in each flower. That's what you get when you take her in: treasures at the end of every stem. And you'll miss it if you don't look. Because not everyone knows how to look into the heart of another person. I just think there is so much to behold in her. She's so faceted, so capable, so thoughtful. I don't know exactly how to express that, but she's not afraid of life, of big thoughts. She's not afraid. She's not gonna run from anything anymore. She's not afraid. I am sorry I didn't look many times, yeah. Too busy, too much wrapped up in my own world. And, what was so important about that world, exactly? I see her now. I can't keep my eyes off of her. She walks into my room and I can't take my eyes off of her. She's a creation of God, created because of our love, Lorrie. Wonderfully made. Wow!

Chase: I always know him as a quiet peace. Cause everybody wants peace and everyone needs someone like Chase. Yeah, I like Chase's peace. He's not demanding something from the space. You can be yourself with Chase. And he's never trying to take something not given. And he doesn't put constants on space and time. There is something magical, something wonderful brewing inside him. Something people want [chuckles]. I don't think he's confused at all. Maybe he's like me; he knows there's treasure and he wants to reveal and share the goods with everyone. Yeah, he does. I think he knows there's some really cool stuff in his inner being. He may not know how to unlock it all yet but when he does, he'll give it up. It's so cool. I missed him once I knew him. I missed not knowing him sooner. Yeah, I did. There is so much to know. Oh, may I be there to know his children, to hold them, like I never got to hold Chase as a boy. Yeah, that's for sure. I love those kids. I do. I sure do.

Margarita: Yes, she is, she is so precious. Margarita has so much joy. She has so much joy. [chuckles] When she looks at those kids, there's so much love. Not just her kids, when she looks at others, she loves. There is, yeah, a love for God that is deep in her, untapped love ready to pour out, like a huge reservoir. She doesn't even know how big it is. Uh, huh. Play with her, spend time with her, the eruption you see when she plays a game is nothing compared to the eruption in the Spirit coming. I pray peace increases in her. It is the road to her reservoir. You can see her when she's at peace, it's written all over her face [chuckles]. Nothing is hidden for her face tells the whole story. Don't you just love that about her? I love to listen to her talk, and tell stories; she is really witty and I love her wit. [chuckles] And she's got a strong sparkle in her eye [chuckles]. She sparkles.

We are so blessed, Lorrie. [chuckles] And, the kids don't even know how much they bless us. They couldn't. I don't want to ruin that. You know what I mean? They just need to be. I just need them to be. That's what blesses me.

Lorrie: [laughing] Oh your smile. Radiates my heart. You have this girlish charm that is irreplaceable. [chuckles] Wow. Charm. You are loaded with charm. Oh my goodness. I've only just begun. You are an explosion of grace and that is so easy to say. You are full of surprises. You are full of grace. It's its own world. Wow. Your grace, it just unfolds and unfolds. I don't even know how to explain what grace means, but I get ever so closer to its definition by watching you and learning from you. The grace I own is because I listened to you. Oh, I just listened. Grace is all about learning for me. We don't get it if we don't learn, no way—because grace is not about ourselves. Oh, we humans are stupid and selfish. I think grace comes from another source, not from ourselves, at least for me it does. Wow, it sure does. It's, oh man, yeah, it's all about coming from another place. It's a mystery; I definitely think it is. I do. Because it's so far from humanity. Just look at our world. The language of grace… we don't know it. It's like it's under lock and key. And you know, it's not of this world because love is not of this world. You can't have grace without love. People have incomplete love without grace. It's missing something, like walking into a beautiful place and not being able to see it all. Whether people are not being open enough not to hear or whatever, if you miss grace you simply cannot love completely.

It was a mystery to me because I was looking too hard into the mirror at myself. There just wasn't enough space in my head. I didn't make space cause I didn't think I could. But there is so much to hear, oh, if you just can make space. Then it's too easy to be arrogant people making everything conform to their own image. They don't look you in the eye. They don't listen. It's all about them. Don't have room for others. But you Lorrie, you made room. You have the lock and the key.

WE DIE

I n February, Darrell and I had decided to rent a large beach house to celebrate Easter with our family and a few friends. It just happened to also be the day of Darrell's and my thirty-fifth wedding anniversary. Several times, I wanted to cancel because of how weak Darrell was becoming, but also kept hoping that we'd have this one last holiday for him and for us. Recognizing how precious and fleeting time was, I didn't want to miss out on making this memory that could turn into strength for our future. Darrell was also determined to celebrate our wedding anniversary. But he was admitted to the hospital again ten days before his death for a series of fluid draining sessions and also more radiation treatment to kill the cancer around his stomach; all of it merely to provide comfort for his last few days.

Darrell began to show some anxiety. His concern was what to expect in the final stage. "I need to speak to a doctor about what this will be like," he said impatiently, asking me to find the attending physician. The doctor relayed some lame course of action to keep him comfortable but didn't say exactly what would happen. That wasn't enough for him. After the doctor left, I told him. "Hon, I don't know, maybe no one does. This I do know. I will be right here experiencing it with you and loving you the whole time." With that, his anxiety eased. "I can't let go of you, Lorrie. I will never let go," he replied. "You are all," he said lovingly to me. He went on. He said, "When life is full of anxiety, there is Lorrie."

It occurred to me after that interaction with Darrell that we must spend our lives learning to let go. When we are young, we think we need to gather things for ourselves, whether possessions, reputations, or people to make our lives complete, but in reality, what makes life complete is relinquishing everything we have taken as our identity that clutters our being. I was his final relinquishment before he was to become solely and completely immersed in eternity.

The most difficult challenge in my life was helping Darrell let go of me. I didn't want to. The thought of it tore at my soul, but I knew I had to try. I had told him a week before this, after watching him suffer, "If you need to go, hon, it's okay. I will be fine." He only replied, "I don't need to go."

The treatments Darrell received in the hospital provided so little comfort that they were hardly worth the trouble and pain. They weakened him further so he could no longer stand or use the restroom independently by mid-April. Then, the doctor ordered some medicine that put him to sleep for three days. The kids and I (and my brother Kevin, who flew in to see Darrell in his last moments) were livid that it stole three days from us. When he woke from that experience, he said, "I feel like I went to hell and back." It felt that way to us too.

> The most difficult challenge in my life was helping Darrell let go of me. I didn't want to. The thought of it tore at my soul, but I knew I had to try.

Darrell was clear after that experience, even asking me to bring his computer so he could finish the reconciliation reports for our non-profit. But he couldn't remember how to log on when we opened the laptop. He kept trying to enter his login information in the Google search box. He wasn't making sense, which frustrated him so. I shut the computer. "We'll work on it later, my love," I said, knowing we may never.

Easter was just days away, and I still hadn't canceled our trip. The attending doctor advised against our plan. When the doctor was talking to us, Darrell seemed to be fading in and out of sleep; but was, in fact, listening to the warnings, the word *eminent* again charged my fear. "This is what I want, yep," Darrell blurts out from no-man's land. The doctor and I snapped our heads to look at this person we thought was asleep but clearly wasn't. Darrell was determined to live at least a few more days. Darrell peeked at us and slowly gave a thumbs-up before drifting off. It was settled: we were going.

It was going to be challenging. The house was on the Eastern Shore, more than an hour away. I needed to rent a reclining wheel-chair for Darrell as well as an SUV to carry it and all the medical supplies. Now that Darrell was immobile, I also needed to arrange transport by ambulance. Leaving him at the hospital to retrieve the wheelchair was excruciating. I worried for him incessantly—that he might die alone. I was also coordinating the food with our friends and our children. I insanely went grocery shopping for what I would cook for Easter. But there was no fooling my reality with would-be normal activity.

I was so anxious that I drove my car into a pole backing up in a parking lot, the second time I wrecked my car in two months. A man who witnessed my pole-bending moment rushed to the car and managed to highlight my wildness. "Whoa, mamma, you gotta be careful," he instructed. "Pftt," is all I could mutter back as I never minded the damage to my car and sped off.

Emergency services were late picking Darrell up, so I followed as night darkened behind the ambulance to meet our family and friends already at the beach house. I was fighting with myself during the drive. Anxiety was hard to tamp down. I could hardly believe I was living these moments in this way. It felt ridiculous. I felt insane.

When we arrived, on April 20th, the welcoming committee was in full force. Darrell was wheeled into the gathering room. It was painfully obvious that he was uncomfortable, squirming in his chair. We could tell he was suffering in both body and mind when he looked at Nancy and demanded she bring him the red cushion (actually the pants she wore that he mistook for a pillow). Then, he demanded to use the restroom but he had a catheter. Unaware and unfiltered he begins to pull his pants down. I raised my voice to him. "No, Darrell, the girls are here?" He pleaded for Jeffrey and Chase to help him, thinking I wouldn't. I rushed to him and pushed him to the bathroom just so he could think he was using the urinal. I held the plastic urinal for him. After a minute, I said,

"How's that, are you finished?" "Yes, thank you," he replied, now relieved of the urge.

We return to a traumatized room, contorted smiles on everyone's face. Absorbing the gravity of the situation was overwhelming for them and terrifying for me. But, Darrell helped ease the trauma of what we all just witnessed by somehow coherently engaging with everyone. I left him with the family to recover myself and set up the bedroom for his care. I had a slew of medical supplies and an air mattress pad that eased the bed sores he had developed from having so little fat left to pad his bones. As I was arranging the bedroom, I heard singing.

I walked out to see that Darrell was leading the group in a worship song. He was clearly the leader, even directing modulations with his upturned hand and pulsing fingers. He messed up the lyrics, but no one cared. They just followed wherever he went. I stood there dazed like suddenly being whiplashed. Darrell was sweet and pure. I was heartened by my loved ones, too, who beautifully accommodated him. The reflections of Darrell's heart were demonstrated to perfection in that act. As much as this trip pushed up against my edges, I was so glad that we were all together to share a love that was thick in that space, in which Darrell could show us his most primitive self. We would face his fate one day ourselves. He was showing us how to die true—and with strength.

The next day, our anniversary and Easter, took all the bravery we could muster. At times it felt like attempting to have a picnic while wild prowlers stalked us. Yet, somehow it was okay. The wheelchair was an epic failure at allowing Darrell to participate. I imagined that we'd get to wheel him to the beach, so he would be able to watch our children and grandchildren do what they do best: play and enjoy each other. But that scenario couldn't play out. He could not get out of bed and didn't even want to try. So, I propped him up in our bedroom, which had big windows looking out to the yard.

I no longer could push away the dreadful reality that Darrell was now actively dying.

We moved all our eating and playing outside to be within his view. I played with the grandkids, so he could see and hear us having fun. Oddly, I was able to enjoy the kids. Truly. We all continued to live, even with the gigantic elephant of mortality breathing down our necks even when we tried to ignore it. The grandkids were a gift for their innocence and energy and pushed back the behemoth just enough for us to realize the day.

When my family all left that evening, I no longer could push away the dreadful reality that Darrell was now actively dying. Our good friend, Deborah, decided to stay with Darrell and me overnight. Darrell's ambulance ride was scheduled for the next day. The plan was to finally set up hospice, which would be ready for him back at our friends' house. Things turned from bad to worse that night. Darrell's breathing became labored. I was panicky he was going to die right there. I turned my body 180 degrees in the bed, so he could see me. I didn't sleep for one second, watching and listening to him breathe. I now had regrets about having come to this beach house. Any confidence I had rigged in my mind that this was a good idea was gone. This was stress. Prayers wouldn't form. All I said was Jesus' name on repeat. All. Night. Long. My prayer was just one name, like a single flare being shot at increasingly desperate intervals into distant heavens.

By mid-morning on April 22ⁿᵈ, the ambulance hadn't come. After franticly calling, I was told they weren't coming due to some insurance issue. I offered to pay whatever it cost. Even so, no emergency vehicles were available. Deborah rushed to the ranger's station and returned with several men who managed to pick Darrell up and place him in Deborah's car because they couldn't get him in the SUV I had rented. It was too high off the ground. Once Darrell had been secured in Deborah's car, one of the older men hugged me. That act of kindness pushed out some of those tears I was holding in. I couldn't afford compassion from anyone. I couldn't fall apart... yet.

Again, I followed behind my man who barely hung on to life. Alone now in my vehicle, tears welled in my eyes just as my friend, Sam, called. Pressurized tears squirted out. "Sam he's dying! Right now he is dying!"

Sam arranged for several men to meet us at the house to get Darrell up the stairs. It was a winding staircase, and any twisting of Darrell's torso put him in extreme pain. "S—t Sam," Darrell yelped to my and everyone's surprise. I wanted to say it too.

The hospice bed was there, along with the nurse, who sat me down at the kitchen table with my daughter and Deborah. She explained what would happen and prescribed the same evil drug that had put Darrell unconscious in the hospital. I did not have that one filled. I didn't want to waste one second more of the life Darrell had left. Besides, he was on morphine and his pain was under control. She warned us about a fish-like gasping for air once death was at the door. I didn't care to hear anymore and left the unhurried nurse with Sarah and Deborah. I rushed to Darrell.

Later that evening, Bill and Nancy joined Darrell and me in the now-hospice-room upstairs. Again, I arranged myself so Darrell could see that I was opposite him. I had my hand on his leg while Bill prayed and affirmed Darrell about what a good friend he was in life, and what a good husband, father, and pastor he was. He spoke of how faithful he was to his life and dreams while I sobbed uncontrollably. Part of me was distressed that Bill was not praying for healing but instead was being benedictory, all too benedictory. I needed the impossible. Just then Darrell raised his arm and suddenly slapped my face, having no strength to control his limbs. He began caressing my cheek with his fingers as Bill's loving prayer continued and I continued to cry. I wasn't doing a good job of helping Darrell let go of me. After Bill and Nancy left, Darrell said cheekily, "Ain't dead yet." He knew my struggle.

Sarah slept with me that night. It was horrid. The breathing machine hospice left was Frankenstein-ish. It whooshed and rattled all night. At 3:30 a.m., I turned it off and tried to adjust Darrell's bed so he wasn't lying on the same part of his body too long. He half joked, "You're gonna make me mad." It must have hurt him somehow; nevertheless, he let me know to stop moving him in his comedic way. I told him that I loved him. He dittoed my confession but his words were not forming well. It sounded like, "I wub oo."

Finally, Sarah and I dozed off. I didn't mean to. Sometime during my sleep of a couple of hours, Darrell became unconscious. I awakened in alarm. Darrell was now breathing in quick gasps from circular lips, the fish-like thing I had hated to learn about. I rushed to use the bathroom. I barely pulled up my pants when I howled across the hall to Jeffrey sleeping in the next room and then back to Sarah, "Wake up! Call Brian, right now. Dad is dying."

Sarah crept to Darrell's side. "Is this it?" she protested, expecting the earth to open or the heavens to flash—something more dramatic for such an excellent man as her father. Darrell breathed two more breaths and not another. "No, no, no, Darrell." I placed my body half over his, no longer worried about hurting him. Why couldn't I transfer my life to his, why wasn't my love powerful enough to bring life back into him? "Come back, come back," I begged. "Remember what we said," I cried. "Please come back!" Still, he didn't breathe. Sarah sobbed. Jeff too. Brian and Chase were on their way. They arrived late. Their eyes were already swollen. Margarita appeared in the doorway after taking the babies to her mom's. She crumbled there and crawled on all fours to Darrell's body, wailing, pulling herself up on the hospice bed rails.

There we all were. Inconsolable. Powerless. Shocked. The six of us stayed with his body for two hours. A friend ventured upstairs and hugged me from behind after the first hour. I had returned to my position lying over Darrell's chest by then. "Come on now, we need to call hospice," she implored. "NO!" We don't," I nearly screamed. She knew. She left me clinging to Darrell. I wasn't ready. This was still my body.

My children remained with me, all on the floor around Darrell. When we gathered our wits, I remembered what Darrell had said about them after Jeffrey's birthday. I retrieved my computer and began to read Darrell's recorded words as he lay there dead. As I read, gratitude spilled out of my children through their tears. I was amazed at how Darrell's impromptu ramblings gave us this seminal moment.

The hospice nurse showed up, anyway. I accepted it. She said she first needed to wash Darrell's body. My kids fled hearing that and descended the stairs into the warm hugs of our friends awaiting them. I stayed. When the nurse rolled Darrell's body to wash his back, the last of my concoctions spilled out of Darrell's mouth. I felt ridiculous and sorry. I suddenly was embarrassed standing before the nurse. It was silly and illogical. Darrell couldn't swallow; yet I had still tried to save him. Even to the end, seeing him dying, my mind couldn't assimilate it. Had I accepted it, I wouldn't have forced my dear man to take in one more drop of any magical potion.

When the nurse finished, I noticed Darrell was wearing one of his favorite t-shirts. I needed it. I asked her to take it off him. I wanted to be alone with Darrell one last time. I closed the door, clinging to his shirt. I knew the funeral director was on his way to take Darrell away, but I needed to have one more conversation with my husband.

"My love, I know we made a deal but it's been three hours now. You must be enjoying your reward. You can let go of me now. I want you to." Just then, in the middle of a cloudless day, the electricity in the room flickered for five seconds or more. I don't know how long really, but it was so profound that I impulsively said, "Is this you?" Was Darrell staying with me until that very moment? I couldn't prove it, yet still, the incident and the energy I felt in that room made the hair stand up on my arms. It was plausible since I believed our spirits are bigger than we are, never limited or weakened by the body or soul.

The funeral director arrived and was overkill on the niceties. He told me he would be my best friend in this process. I wasn't feeling it: I didn't need a best friend in him. All I saw was his way-too-white, extra wide smile coming at me. Why I noticed it was odd, but it took up space in my mind that I didn't want to share with him. I had no patience for the shiny-toothed man. He was the one who was going to put my husband into a body bag and no horse smile coming at me was going to help that searing fact. He asked me to leave and wait downstairs. I obliged because this was one thing of all the merciless things I experienced, I didn't want to see.

I joined my family and friends on the porch. A few minutes later, the door opened. Darrell was zipped up a black bag and being pushed out on a gurney. I heard a symphony of gasps from my children next to me. We watched as the funeral director and another worker struggled to get the gurney down the stairs from the porch to the sidewalk. The crude rocking and clanking of the gurney amplified my eerie mood. Darrell was then carted to the curb and loaded into the back of a hearse. I rushed to it as it drove away.

> I had no patience for the shiny-toothed man. He was the one who was going to put my husband into a body bag...

I watched the hearse turn to leave the neighborhood. Stunned, I turned to my family standing a few yards behind me. We stared at each other; no one moved. What now? I looked deeply at them and tried to walk. I couldn't move. It was as if I had suddenly seen a venomous snake and froze from fright as I did once as a young girl when my family camped on the Colorado River. I was stuck inside my body. My wits were nowhere to be found.

Later, my children and I gathered ourselves and drove to the funeral home. We learned what was going to happen to Darrell's body. We talked about a funeral. I knew I wanted an open casket. It was hard for my psyche to accept Jeff's death back in 1982 because I never saw him dead, nor did I attend the burial. Repeat nightmares of Jeff being a zombie and having to protect him tortured me for months on end in the early days of my first widowhood. It was only when I drove back to the accident site in the desert and had touched the ruins from that day—pieces of the car and a lone red sock of my infant son—did that nightmare stop. I didn't want others to experience anything like that. I wanted my children to have the opportunity for their brains to accept his death. Besides, a funeral allows for the power of legacy and gratitude to arise.

We were given instructions by the gracious assistant to the shiny-toothed man. My friend, Deborah, served us by keeping us on task since the kids and I walked around stunned with slowed reactions and comprehension. The viewing and funeral were scheduled for the next week. It was too soon; we didn't allow enough time for family and friends to arrive. Plus, there was much to do in that short time. I was obsessed with getting a memorial video done, but I couldn't access our photos and movies, which were all back home—four hours away. But, somehow, Sarah and her friend managed to pull it off with the photos some friends were able to round up.

The beauty of that week was everywhere. Loved ones served my children and me, donated money for expenses, embraced us in hugs, provided meals, and worked to set up the viewing by having Darrell's nature photography framed. Rather than flowers, I asked that donations be made to our non-profit to help me finish our work.

The funeral was intimate, with each of our children and Darrell's brother, Jeff, speaking beautifully. They had people laughing one second and pierced through the heart the next. When my turn came to speak, I didn't know if I could. I stood but hesitated. Once I put one foot in front of me, I was committed. I had no prepared notes, but after hearing others speak about Darrell's praise-worthy attributes, I realized that those weren't what I loved most. What I prized was his struggle. I wanted to tell that side of him because it was his greatest love gift to me, our children and his God. He didn't allow the demons of having an absent, alcoholic, Native American father to define his personality forever. He had fought hard for us. It gifted me with a hard-won love affair that lasted until the very end. That was the essence of my tribute. He was my hero for becoming all that he was. I was relieved that I didn't ugly-cry or cry much at all. I felt proud of my children and the family we still were. My children were beautiful, raw, and authentic.

I stood there, thinking that not only was he gone, but *we* were too. We died.

It wasn't until the burial that I broke down. Walking away from Darrell's casket after the graveside service was impossible. If it weren't for my sons surrounding me and helping me walk, I would have collapsed. Halfway to the car I did, but their bodies and arms created a basket of love for me to fall into.

We immediately went to a luncheon with the family and all the out-of-town guests. I was numb. I managed to visit but was increasingly agitated. I couldn't wait for lunch to be over for one reason: I needed to return to the cemetery. I asked Chase if he and Sarah would take me. I didn't tell them why. Chase just lovingly did what I had asked. When we arrived, I rushed to the burial plot alone. I nursed the illogical hope that Darrell could still come back and would need someone to let him out of that darn box. It sounded like a horror scene, yet, my wild imagination coerced me.

Oh no! I gasped. Darrell was already in the ground; several feet of fresh dirt now sealed him in. He did not need me anymore. He was never coming back. I stood there, thinking that not only was he gone, but *we* were too. We died.

LOOKING
FOR RELICS

"We still want you to come, Lorrie," my dear friend Diane entreated about a trip to Italy that Darrell and I had planned on taking at the end of June of 2019 with her and her husband, Dave, and a group of friends, including Bill and Nancy. Of course, no one knew that Darrell would be gone when he planned it. Now, I worried I'd be the grieving widow and weigh down my would-be happy vacationing friends.

Then, another set of friends, Chris and Deborah, called. They had the wild idea for me to go on a family vacation to Scotland with them and their girls the first week of June. "No, Deb. I will ruin your vacation," I repeated the excuse I had given Diane. It hadn't even been a month since Darrell had passed when she first asked. "We want you to ruin our vacation," she cheekily but seriously replied to my brush-off. After a few days, I changed my mind. My work and the TV series found their origins in England. I imagined seeing the places I'd written about, and someone thought it might be possible to do more research.

I also had a hint of hope that my now shaky faith might be steadied and my dashed sense of my purpose sorted. But God was noticeably silent. The atmosphere seemed stale, filled with old hope and old faith. It was unpleasant to breathe it, as compared to the previous months when divine comfort had been fresh every day. At least for Darrell, it was. I tapped his faith in those days when mine was flitting around—one-minute praying fierce prayers for healing—and the next minute trying to find faith to brave his looming death.

The Italy part of the trip had a first leg in Oxford, England, toward the end of June, because Bill taught and guided a C.S. Lewis class and tour every year. I would have a solo adventure for ten days in between Scotland and meeting up with friends in Oxford before we flew to Florence. When I told my children I was going to travel to Scotland and tour through the United Kingdom's countryside by myself before flying to Italy, some thought I was being reckless. The condition for my going was they had to have access to my location, using my shared location app on my phone at all times. Okay, deal.

I landed in Edinburgh on June 5th with my first set of friends, Chris and Deborah, and their girls, Emma and Sofie. We took off from there and toured the countryside, traveling in our Mercedes rental van. The beauty of Scotland was stunning. Interestingly enough, Darrell's favorite flower, the foxglove, was in bloom literally wherever there was dirt. From valleys to cliffs, these stalks of flowering bells met my gaze. I made it a mission to take as many photos of them as possible. I didn't entertain them as a sign or anything transcendent. They were simply a lovely memento of my beloved so recently taken away. Besides, at this point, consolation prizes for my loss were not good enough.

It was like I was saying to God, "Don't go being nice now." I couldn't think like others that Darrell was in the butterflies or birds, or even the lizard that hung out with my daughter and me the day after the funeral when she took me to the beach. I never chided anyone's earnest desire to know that Darrell was still with us, having been humiliated by my fairytale thinking. It was a weird phenomenon and now a waste of my emotions. It simply was not where I wanted my mind to go. It didn't help me, and I didn't want a replacement lizard.

I hoped that I wasn't turning cynical, but I did have the sense that I held diminished space for God, while at the same wanting to know him in a different dimension. I was confused, fickle, and demanding. But, that was me: needing him but being troubled by him. It was like standing at the edge of my future and wanting to hide already. Uncharted territory was no longer a thrill but dark and ugly from all the indifference the world seemingly rained down on me. I needed to find beauty again, wherever it might be found.

If, by chance, these adventures would include being interrupted by the Lord of Creation while my friends were my only connection to him, I hoped he might. I needed him to. I was a bit afraid that it wasn't just the world that was unsympathetic, but perhaps God was too. I needed more than a flower or animal—and more than Darrell in any illusory form. I needed my doubts transcended and my overwhelming emptiness to be filled. I wondered how that could happen, the pit in me was massive. Besides, it appeared I might be stepping into my future with a naughty list tucked away. It had a singular entry. It read, "Lorrie's Naughty List: God Almighty." I hoped my demands at least humored him just as my children did me when they refused a smile in order not to yield; yet all the while, they hoped I was watching them languish, anyway. The unseemly part of my attitude was that I was in my fifties and still sufficiently skillful at that game.

> ... it appeared I might be stepping into my future with a naughty list tucked away. It had a singular entry. It read, "Lorrie's Naughty List: God Almighty."

The tour in Scotland was lovely. I enjoyed myself and my company. I even thought I contributed to the fun, especially in our very long towing expedition to Inverness after blowing out a couple of tires in the middle of the Highlands. We ate fabulous food, hiked, saw the most breathtaking sites and castles, learned history, and laughed a lot. Debbie and the family doted on me constantly. I felt loved and didn't cry... noticeably.

My friends took off for home early on June 15, 2019, from the airport in Edinburgh. Suddenly I felt anxious. I pulled the covers over my head in the hotel and tried to sleep some more. I couldn't. I wondered if it was a terrible mistake to stay in the UK alone. I had to talk to myself; I had to remember. I had taken people around the world before, even to some dangerous places, and never once was I afraid. I reminded myself of what people saw in me and how my husband was always reeling me in from my risk-taking ways. After a fiery pep talk I had with myself in my bed sheet cave, I rushed out of the hotel to rent my five-speed, metallic orange Mini.

Before leaving Scotland, I visited the Museum of Edinburgh just because it would have been a shame not to. I was feeling more courageous as I headed south on my way to Oxford. I didn't have a plan mapped out. I had a bucket list of places I wanted to see, but other than that, I didn't feel any need to keep to a schedule. "Take that Darrell," I laughed, remembering his partiality to sticking to a schedule, especially when navigating from one location to the next. I only knew that I eventually needed to meet up in Oxford with Dave, Diane, Bill, and Nancy. On my way from Edinburgh to my first bucket list stop, Hadrian's Wall, I found a bed and breakfast.

I arrived at this beautiful converted castle. It happened that I was the only guest that night. My room was exquisite and timeless, very feminine in the sense of its floral ascetics, but I knew it would have also been inviting for Darrell still. I lay on the bed not sure what to do. I gazed out the window at the vast gardens and distant landscape. I felt so alone in that moment but refused to give in to tears. Debbie left me her violet gin. I hoped a straight shot of it would put me to sleep. It took two (or maybe three), but I slept. I rose the next morning to a dining room set for a queen, yet it was only me. I was cared for and served as if I were nobility.

I sat there alone, taking it all in, and suddenly remembered a scene from a daydream I had when Darrell had his breakdown those many years ago. Darrell had lost a large portion of his memory. He was agitated and incapable of a meaningful conversation. During that confusing time, one day I was driving down the highway and saw a picture in my mind's eye of a cloud of witnesses peering through Heaven, cheering for what I thought must be us (Darrell and me). But suddenly, in that daydream, I distinctly knew that wasn't it. It was as if I had heard, "It's you."

I was being challenged to believe that I am valued and cheered as an individual and a woman. I made a declaration in my soul that day. It turned out to be the key to exiting fear. It included a confession that, no matter what happens, even if Darrell never comes back to me or as the same man, I will be fine. I will be loved and thrive in my life.

Another memory zoomed by. I had the same rare experience of needing to make a confession about myself living in an unforgiving world. Jeffrey was a baby and I feared that he would be left severely disabled or worse. I wanted to relinquish him into the Lord's care but couldn't fully. I had worked very hard to analyze and understand Jeffrey's brain injury to make sure he'd flourish in life. While that sounded noble, underneath my motivation was the belief that I might not get the outcomes I wanted and that my faith alone wasn't going to save him. My labors were tinged with unbelief, no matter how gallant my determination was. It's not that they weren't useful. They were. It's just that my efforts needed an infusion of peace. What I had to settle was the question that even if Jeffrey didn't recover or he died, as his father had, would I be okay. That was a harsh reckoning; I couldn't imagine it. Then, after a long, tearful wrestling over the act of relinquishment on the balcony of my parents' condo in Honolulu, I was able to say, and mean it, that I trusted that I'd be okay, no matter the aftermath. It changed me.

So, it was just me, in that dining room, being served and cared for. The thought of both confessions made years ago pushed a few tears from my eyes as I sat in that historic room, deciding which utensil to use for my fruit. The emotion came strong; I perfectly remembered how it had felt and how the soul can so easily refuse to be comforted. The exercise of letting go is ridiculously hard. It costs something.

I took it in, not knowing what it meant. I didn't want to know what it would cost if I were to face the Lord square as I had in those moments when sacrifice felt unfair and impossible. But, I left the castle in my Mini a little lighter in my soul. I even found myself humming as I zipped around the countryside. When I caught myself doing it, I was stunned. I had only ever caught myself randomly humming while painting. Once.

I made it to Hadrian's Wall mid-afternoon. It was a bucket list item because some ten years previous, when Darrell and I were in the North of England, we had a mutual unspoken curiosity about this broken red line on our map marked "Hadrian's Wall." All I had known was that Hadrian was a Roman Emperor. I had thought to myself that we needed to go there when I saw it, but we had no time, needing to make a flight from London that evening. As we drove to London, Darrell blurted out, "We need to go to Hadrian's Wall and shout "freedom." Without hesitation, I said, "I know!" I had meant going to the wall; I wasn't sure about the "freedom" part. My husband was the dramatic one and only he would think in *Braveheart* fashion. This was one of the few peculiar moments we had in our joint Seed of a Nation mission, where we became aware that there was something we needed to know more about, without knowing what it was, much less why it mattered.

When we returned to the States the next day to pick up our vehicle from our friend, Irv, he handed us a book that he thought we would like. It was a work someone had just given him entitled *Hadrian's Wall*. What? Hadrian's Wall! We looked at each other, astonished and compelled. That entire Hadrian's Wall experience opened a whole new vantage point for the Penn story we had yet to incorporate. It eventually caused us to realize that we had only touched the surface of a message we were speaking already.

I saw the wall as I was driving to my next lodging. I pulled off the road where there was a historic Roman temple, but there was no clear access. Yet, it was clearly in the distance. Since I was going to attempt Darrell's shout of freedom into the atmosphere—for God knows what good—I thought this would be the spot since the only living things around were a few sheep. I don't shout. I don't shout well, anyway. Even when I tried to yell at my children when they were young, they learned to say, "Try again, Mom." (They playfully tease me about it to this day.)

I took off for the wall through a pasture. Halfway there, I thought there had to be a better way to reach it since I was constantly dodging sheep poop and mud. But I kept going; I was too vested by then. At one point, about fifty yards from the wall, I didn't realize that the deeper mud was a soggy bog. My right leg sank up above my knee. I wiggled my leg and the suction released it. I was glad that my shoe was tightly knotted. I was definitely not turning back now—otherwise, the bog would have won. I carried on, climbing a hill to make it to the ruins, only to discover that I was standing on the remains of an old house or barn, not Hadrian's Wall. Defeated, I trekked back to my car, mud bespattered, even on my face. Adopting a Lewis and Clark determination, I resolved to find the real structure before nightfall.

I drove another five miles and found a clearly-marked touristy location. It was getting dark and it began to rain, but it was of no matter now. I was, in fact, in great need of a shower anyway. I walked down a grassy slope. It was slick as ice. I fell twice. Both mishaps produced a feet-up-in-the-air thud. Yet my doggedness drove me to complete my mission. I thought maybe I could shout now that a fight with nature and my bloopers instigated me.

Then, I found it. I finally climbed onto the three-foot-wide remains of Hadrian's Wall. I scanned the landscape, making sure I didn't see people. I felt a bit foolish, which provoked my laugh-cry emotion to erupt to the surface. My first attempt was feeble and ridiculous. A baby, "freedom," escaped, not enough to even bother the lambs. But then, I got louder; as I did my voice started cracking and a tear leaked out. My sheepy audience slowly turned their heads, seemingly puzzled by me; I imagined them echoing my children, "Try again, lady." My vocal failure strangely embarrassed me. There were no people nearby. I felt similarly in the past when my tone-deaf singing had ruined a song. It was just the sheep and me staring at each other over my thwarted shout, which ushered in nothing noticeable from Heaven but perhaps more rain. Nah, it was going to rain, anyway. I produced nothing. I hoped Darrell got to peek at this; it now felt like he punked me into it. That thought made me sigh and then chuckle. What did we think we'd accomplish on this wall? It was now pouring rain on my head; at least the mud on my face washed off.

I made another attempt during this journey to dredge the past that Darrell and I had had. Years before, our British friend, Roger, took Darrell and me to George Fox's Pulpit in Cumbria County, North England. While there, Darrell and Roger prayed endlessly. Roger said prayers came easy there since it was a location where beautiful things happened in people's lives. It was where George Fox, the founder of the Quakers, preached to thousands in the seventeenth century and where many reportedly had radical spiritual and healing experiences. So the day after the parody on Hadrian's Wall, I drove myself through familiar narrow hedge rows, backing up twice for at least twenty-five yards for oncoming traffic.

Once I had found the site, I again dodged animal poop while climbing around the rural amphitheater. There were no ethereal, wild horses with manes flowing to the ground appearing like the time before. There was no weighty divine presence making it easy to pray. I was scarcely inspired. The only thought I could muster to say was, "Well, this isn't it." What exactly I wanted to happen, I didn't know. I could check this effort off the list. It seemed looking for relics of us wasn't working.

Interestingly enough, I wasn't disheartened—feeling a bit ridiculous, yes. It was my adventure; my silver lining was feeling empowered and confident. I felt reluctant to push off from my grief, to journey too far past Darrell and our life. Doing so seemed to diminish what we had had as if it didn't matter, like we were a blip. Letting new happen sometimes seemed like forcing Darrell further into the background. How could all the power that was us fall to the ground? We had built something together; we demonstrated rebirth, passion, and real cause. Our marriage was renewed time and again along with our joint mission in life, which was much bigger than us individually. I wanted to honor us but was left with unanimated relics of our love and life. It would take work and hoopla to sell, even to myself, that the past had enough power for the future.

> I felt reluctant to push off from my grief, to journey too far past Darrell and our life. ... I wanted to honor us but was left with unanimated relics of our love and life.

Somehow, I knew my experiences in the past could only inform me. As much as I tried to recreate experiences, the past wasn't porting over those happy-good feelings. The effort left me wanting. The taste of sarcasm over the idea that Darrell would be with in some capacity grew stronger. My mind wasn't geared to believing he could comfort me still and yet I didn't want to be alone and without him. What was I to do? That question was too complex to reconcile in the moment. My traveling partially acquitted me from the hard work of figuring out what my options were. None were evident.

My toil at that very moment was to venture forth in the heart-ache that reminded me that Darrell would never do any of this with me. Ever. Again. Somehow those thoughts felt like running over hot coals while trying not to be burned. So, I didn't pause further thinking about them. I zoomed off to my next bucket list item: Swarthmore Hall in Ulster. Darrell and I had never been there, but I had written about it. It was a setting in a scene in my Penn TV series.

A GLIMPSE OF
TRANSCENDENCE

Angelic choral music rose through my Elizabethan window at Swarthmore Hall almost immediately after I had settled in my room. I opened the historic diamond-paned windows to hear it better. A rehearsal was taking place in an outbuilding to my manor, which had been half converted to a bed and breakfast. The other half remained just as it was when it was the home of Margaret Fell-Fox, a prominent 17th-century figure in my writings. The music was like nothing I had ever heard before: it was ethereal. I had the same feeling the first time I heard Andre Bocelli in concert. The purity of his voice danced around in my soul with the effect of producing tears.

I was given equal access to the home's untouched historic side. Over the two days I was there, I would bring my morning coffee into the dining room and sit where I imagined my characters to be convening for meals and meetings, which in those days repeatedly landed Quakers in miserable prisons just for the act of gathering in crowds of more than five people. I also spent time in what was George Fox's[7] old bedroom where I found original writings to read. I wandered the estate, absorbing the environment and reliving the scenes I wrote. It was a storyteller's and historian's wonderland. I loved every minute in those spaces.

On the second day, a Quaker service was held in the dining room. I went out of curiosity. It turned out that I was the only guest—just me and a kind maternal Quaker woman. We made small talk. I told her this location was on my husband's and my bucket list. I also told her of the significance of its historical context to me. But, of course, there was no husband with me, which begged her question. Once she learned that I was recently widowed, she merely looked at me and said, "My dear, you are in need of some care." She immediately got up and found a wool blanket to cover my lap before giving me a few instructions as we sat in antique chairs next to each other.

We were to sit silently and meditate to quiet ourselves to either hear from God or just center our souls. We did that. Even before I closed my eyes, I felt tears brimming my eyelids. Talking about my loss to a welcoming soul took down my defenses, allowing grief to rush forward. At first, all I could think about was controlling

---

7   George Fox was the founder of the Quakers. In 1669 he married Margaret Fell, a prominent widow with significant social standing. She was an early convert to Quakerism.

my thoughts to stop the tears, but those tears came hot and fast. I just tried hard not to make a noise that would interrupt my new friend's focus. I didn't blow my nose or suck anything back in. Goo and tears littered my face, ran over my lips, and down my neck. I tried to scoop it up in my hands, but then what to do with it? I gave in. I let it happen and hoped that before she opened her eyes, I could retrieve a tissue. As moments passed, however, I forgot about my lack of decorum and just emptied myself into the experience. It was a useless effort at that point, anyway. I wept quietly. Halfway through, I felt light shining on my face as the sunlight came through the aged, leaded glass. The passing minutes turned peaceful, even with my continuing tears.

After twenty minutes, my compassionate new friend opened her eyes and spoke. She already had a tissue ready. She looked long into my eyes and said, "As I thought about you, I saw dappling light shine on your face. Does that mean anything?" It didn't really, but I had felt it. I immediately snapped my head toward the windows only to realize that the windows were behind me and to the far-right side. I pondered the source of the light, then slowly turned my head back to resume our conversation. I didn't know what to think and dismissed it. Nonetheless, I was grateful for her compassion. She then took me to the kitchen to brew me some tea. We visited for a few more minutes. She introduced me to the staff after I became composed. From then on, they all looked out for me and helped me when I was searching for a piece of context for my story.

When the staff learned of my project, they recommended I spend time at Woodbrooke in Birmingham, the international Quaker college and research center. Since I was winging it anyway, that became my next stop. I had to drive through the Lake District on my way to Birmingham and found a boutique hotel to stay at near Lake Windermere next to the Great Knott Wood. While walking to find dinner that night, I stopped to read a marker about the woodland I was passing by. It showed twisty-barked trees called yews. I decided that the next morning I would hike to find one of these trees.

I rose early and eager the following day to adventure into the Great Knott Wood. The beauty of the spring forest and the activity helped soothe a nagging loneliness that had returned to me the night before. It was the kind of sadness that comes unannounced and with an inconvenient lump in the throat. Again, I saw foxglove plants blooming everywhere, some taller than me. I took more pictures since that was my assumed job description at the time. I also took photos of bright yellow fungi, wild mushrooms, fallen moss-covered trees, and ancient stone walls. Yet, I couldn't find any yews. I traipsed on. I was running out of time to check out of my room, so I hurried. When I thought I needed to admit defeat, I turned a corner and saw a sign welcoming me to the "dappling light."

Dappling. Light!? The rush of my Quaker friend's words reverberated in my head. I knew what the word dappling meant, but I hadn't heard it used much over the years and now twice within days. I arrested my attention and I stood staring at the sign. The thing was, I had noticed the light dancing around the wood as I hiked. It was beautiful how the sun shone on the ground in bits and pieces as the gentle breeze moved the leaves in the canopy aside. But now I could name it: it was a thing. It was the dappling-light-thing my brain was set to identify and now prioritize. I quickly turned around to head back. Just then, I saw it. The yew tree was up on the hill in front of me. Freshly queued, I noticed the dappling light too, highlighting moss-topped stones like stair-steps to the magical tree where pixies might play.

I had to get closer. There were actually two yews next to each other. One had a low branch precisely the correct height for a bench, inviting me to sit. I did. I watched the light bounce down the fuzzy green branch. It led my eyes outward beyond the tip to the most brilliant meadow. The light was so bright that it looked fake. I sat there and took it in. Suddenly I burst into tears, thoughts slowly following. It was as if that meadow were a promise, and the bits of light were going to lead me to it one day.

Finally, I was courageous enough to speak words to God. I hadn't uttered his name since Darrell had died (although I covertly wanted to know if he saw me). I was compelled to say something. I remembered what Darrell had said to me as he was dying when he spoke of worship being spontaneous, involuntary even, and how his suffering brought clarity and meaning to it like he had never known. In that forest, I realized that I was being invited to find him anew in my suffering. If ever my spirit were primed to respond by circumstances and creation, it was then. It went simply like this, "Okay. If you can give me enough light for each moment, each hour, each day, it will be sufficient." It was so hard to say. I wept doing it but I also felt my words pierced a barrier to trust.

If I had an actual naughty list, I would have left it there with my tree. It was not because I could claim any victory over suffering—I knew I had a long way to go—but because I was willing to move into the light, to let go, to see things differently. I was willing to feel.

I made it to Birmingham after a couple of days and after stopping at several castles—forgotten ones and touristy ones too. My family traces its lineage on my mother's French side back to William the Conqueror; perhaps something in me connected to the land that I loved so much driving through. I mastered roundabouts and dodging sheep in villages while driving on the left side of the road. These were my new skills.

Once checked into my Woodbrooke dorm room, I began exploring the library. Their original works were impressive. I felt like a student again: it suited me. I met some folks there. One man named Stuart encouraged me more than he knew. After spending time with another staff member, I was asked if I would consider doing my PhD there. The thought enticed me, but I knew what would happen. It would be all I would do for my next years. It would make sense to those watching, and it would produce pre-dictable outcomes. It would give me credibility and open doors in a few arenas. I knew I could do it, and more… I could love it. But, I wanted to get this story told to as many people as possible, however risky a feature or television series would be in terms of financial and emotional investment. But life is risky. I never minded the invita-tion. I was going to try to finish what I had started.

I made it to Oxford and united with my friends, Bill, Nancy, Dave and Diane. I made some new friends too. I didn't participate much in the C.S. Lewis tour. I wasn't quite ready for groups of strangers. Instead, I obtained a temporary library card to use the Bodleian Library; in my imagination, it was the ultimate research facility and where I wished I had access to all these years.

One evening out for dinner, my new friend, Cynthia (also wid-owed), met a group of single men having dinner near our table. She struck up a conversation with them. They invited her to an after-dinner event. Rushing back to our table in hopes of gathering up the only other single girl, me, she implored me to join her. I must have looked shocked because Nancy grabbed my arm as if to say, "You don't have to go." "I know," I whispered back without a look. I declined Cynthia by saying, "Another time." After she bounded off, I posed a question to my table of friends, "What if some guy wanted to talk?" I was imagining it. "How does that conversation go when he finds out I've been a widow for only two months? And twice at that. Uh, no!" My friends smiled sympathetically but their controlled faces said they were also amused.

Before the flight to Italy, I wanted to visit a few historic sites near London. I wanted to connect with the producer I had met in February. I left Oxford for a last lone adventure. It kept me from dealing with the emptiness of the haunting next day: Darrell's fifty-ninth birthday. It would be my first celebration day without him. Darrell loved birthdays so much that he practically planned his own. He wasn't shy about it, either. Everyone who knew him would have no doubt what kind of cake to bring. If I had ever yelled out in a room full of his peeps the question of what cake we should have for him, they would say loudly in unison, "Chocolate!"

I arrived at the hotel room that night after first visiting the poet John Milton's 17th-century cottage. I already had a mini-meltdown while driving, thinking about Darrell's birthday. Once in the room, the magnitude of missing him crudely slapped me. I was proud of myself for successfully navigating my European adventure intact, with confidence and even enjoyment. Suddenly, my pulse raced, pushing faster and faster as grief erased the hopefulness I gained. I felt every shard of heartbreak as I sobbed into the hotel pillow. I was trying to live like Darrell had wanted, like he had made me promise to do. But the pain of doing it was the centerfold in my thoughts. So many ups and downs wearied me and now I was like,

"What's the point of seeing another beautiful sunrise if I couldn't do it with him?" The next morning I wrote him a letter; it took that heaviness off me for the time being:

> Happy Birthday, my darling!
>
> Today we were supposed to fly to Italy together to celebrate with friends. But, you are nowhere, and yet, everywhere—all at the same time. In these past two months and a few days, it was you who naggingly replaced an "Oh no!" each morning with your exhortation, "I need you to live."
>
> It's you who reoriented me to invite and capture beauty rather than succumb to a seducing asceticism just there. It's you who made me share my ramblings with my friends as a discipline for my life and a defiance of earthy death, for you knew what would be necessary when it just got too loud.
>
> It's you whose struggle to shed self was your greatest love gift to your God, me, and our children. For in that ongoing act, you taught us how to live and also how to die gracefully, embracing two realities at once.
>
> It's you whose love, so thorough, leaves no void wanting except for your presence. It turns the ridiculous claim that you'll always be with me into a real possibility. For you, and your more-than-merrier attitude, I celebrate! In public, no less. So, if you can peek through the cloud of witnesses to see me wandering the planet without you, you know what that means.
>
> I miss you, Lorrie

And that was that. I needed to engage with life, and I did. The next day, I was in a montage of activities. I drove to the school (still in operation) where a main character in my project attended. I received a proper scolding for showing up while classes were in session. It was entirely worth the rebuke. I was met at the studio lot, where the producer I had been to see before Darrell had passed has offices. They gave me the whole tour, which included picture taking where Master Chef was filmed. Soon after, I met up with my USA friends at the airport.

Italy was spectacular, even more so because of the extravagant kindness of my beloved friends. I felt every minute of the trip from cruises, hikes, and train rides along rugged terraced coastlines with its centuries-old, colorful houses in Cinque Terra to adventures through Tuscany's vineyard and a week in Florence. The Uffizi Gallery was overwhelming. I spent five hours surrounded by some of the most important pieces of art dating from the Renaissance.

The food and the wine were life-changing at Dave's and Diane's restaurant, Brandolino's, which just so happened to have been one of Medici's private chapels, now converted. Stories of the old world spoke to me through distressed walls and buttressed arches. Our dinners were long-evening events, every night while in Florence. Even the Michelin Star Restaurant on the Italian Riviera paled in comparison to Brandolino's. I would leave Italy a wine snob and black truffle addict after experiencing my first eyes-rolling-back-into-my-head taste of Brandolino's truffle pasta.

Beyond all that, no one let me pay for a thing except for gifts to take home. I only cried once in front of my friends and it was my fault for asking a street musician to play the last songs Darrell had dedicated to me. I almost immediately regretted inserting drama into our group walkabout that night. It felt indulgent once the song triggered tears. Nonetheless, my friends were gracious. Diane even bought me a rose which became a prop for picture taking.

On the last day in Florence, I strolled alone in an Italian marketplace and stopped to enjoy my last cappuccino. I felt overwhelmingly privileged that I could be doing just that. I observed the passersby feeling content. I was not necessarily engaged with the world or wanted to be, yet I didn't feel aloof, either. I thought this was what neutral feels like. I felt safe with my friends. And I felt noticeably safe sitting there alone, taking up solitary space. I reveled a bit. Not knowing what was ahead was too big of a thought for contemplation, so I didn't bother because in that very minute, I was good. In that very moment, I experienced Lorrie. I was not Lorrie and Darrell. I was not Lorrie, the mother. I was not Lorrie, the good girl always holding my motives to account. I was just me, allowed to take up space just because that space was singularly mine.

In significant ways, that sense of being in the stillness of my heart felt like a promise equal to the one I had sung to my three-month-old son all those years back after struggling so hard to trust. I was given bursts of light then and now again, it seemed. First through my friends, then through my new experiences. I didn't know what shape my faith would take now. It was conveniently vague. But, I knew it was going to be, and needed to be, different. Just as I delighted to reveal myself to my children in a game of hide and seek, maybe God might pop out of nowhere along the way. I felt a rush of curiosity about how he might.

The worst was yet to come for me in my journey to wholeness. Emotional regulation was going to be hard and embarrassing as events would unfold. But those few weeks in Europe elevated me just enough above the crush to gain some perspective. The unconditional love of friends and the beauty of creation that spoke to me in a language surpassed understanding. I felt its impact and somehow in the sum of all the past weeks, it equaled hope. It rang true and was the biggest reason for my gratitude as I sat at that café; it was consistent with my personhood.

> The unconditional love of friends and the beauty of creation that spoke to me in a language surpassed understanding.

I never was very good at adhering to set patterns, which at best were a framework but incapable of gathering my fortitude enough to have me obey its rules or religious traditions. My resolve had to spring from a substance I could qualify as life-giving. It had to be transcendent. I had read and believed that is why God's affirming nature was revealed to humankind in the first place: so the mundane wouldn't be all there is. It suited me and the organic approach to life that I wanted. In my mind, there was no point to my having faith if it weren't animated. That was my worry after Darrell died. How to have confidence and be present to life seemed a steep ask. I had the same question after Jeff died, too, when I wondered if divine grace were sufficient for peace and vitality. All I had for now was this trip and a glimpse of transcendence. If it remained so, I could navigate life. Alone. I hoped.

THE FIRST YEAR

Coming home after my trip felt like running into barbed wire. A series of challenging events hacked at my recently gained confidence and ended up complicating my grief journey. Some of it could be expected, and some of it was truly mind-bending. Remarkably, I kept my energy up for all that needed to be accomplished; my strength lasted through the next ten months—and then, it dissolved.

It all began with me finally driving home to the mountains. I had been back only once, for a day, in the last nine months. I knew I had to start packing and move to the beach where my children and grandchildren lived. The work was the least of my concerns. The next few days would be the last time I would occupy the space my husband and I freely shared. It would be haunting. I caught myself holding my breath the closer I approached our home on the four-hour drive.

When I pulled into the driveway of our home, images of Darrell flashed by. He was in the garden just beyond the hood of my car. He was there in the creative landscaping so naturally fitted to the mountain we lived on. His last motions assaulted my senses. I saw him moving boulders from their God-given placement on the planet to Darrell's decidedly more perfect spot. He towed them on a makeshift sled behind the riding lawn mower, always reminding me of Mr. Magoo, especially when he waved to me as he putted by the widow of our bedroom.

My hands trembled while inserting the key into the door. Inside, I stood out of proportion to the room, my soul taking up more space than my body. Everything swirled in deafening silence: there was his denim jacket hanging over a chair, the fur pillows he had me make, the walking sticks he had carved, and his books. I saw him there. I remembered the signature twinkle in his eyes and the wide smile he so naturally formed upon seeing me. I knew his passion to make me happy. I experienced the beauty and pain of his vulnerability. One of my friends asked me while in Italy if there was anything I wished I had said to my husband and hadn't. There wasn't. We had no unspoken words, no regrets unreconciled, nor pain not embraced. Now those life-giving memories were being cannibalized by ghosts. Those opaque images of Darrell were everywhere.

I felt frozen lying in our bed, as if nightfall was just there, waiting to extract marrow from my bones. Strange sounds hurled fear like stalking entities. Being on that mountain by myself now intimidated me: that was new. I had always savored time alone in that house when Darrell traveled, never once being fearful.

Now those life-giving memories were being cannibalized by ghosts. Those opaque images of Darrell
were everywhere.

The next morning, I started searching the internet for a home
in Virginia Beach where my family lived. My children and two
grandchildren fastened me to a semblance of my life. Besides, we
found strength in our togetherness. But first, I needed to evaluate
my financial situation to make the move. I knew we had depleted
our funds to launch our projects and spent massive amounts of
money to save Darrell's life.

Darrell had for the last two decades managed our finances. I
hoped I'd find help for a down payment on a home with his life
insurance policies. He had passed so quickly; we hadn't talked about
how I was to live after that event. Besides, I didn't think he would
be taken from me. When I realized that he might, he couldn't talk
about it. His stop-looking-at-me-like-I-am-dead comment pre-
cluded us from talking about life insurance, except once during
the week before he died when I asked him where he had those
files. By then, however, he couldn't evoke the past; those memories
seemed cut off from him. In that time, I watched him live minute
by minute like each one was the alpha and omega of his entire life.
In those moments, the past didn't exist. Or, maybe it was that the
past did not matter anymore. What he did recall and verbalize was
the love he felt for the people in his life. That's it.

I found multiple policies in a portable file box Darrell had
stored away. I called each company. I was shaken to find that only
one was valid, and it wasn't going to be enough. Three term policies had lapsed. For the first time since he passed, I was angry with

him… and myself for not paying attention. I kept looking for a home, anyway. I had specific needs: the first was having a garage. Darrell and I still had most of our household from our last six-bedroom home in Pennsylvania in storage. I knew sorting through all our stuff would exact emotional energy and having the garage was key to allowing me to accomplish it slowly. I also knew I needed to bring Jeffrey with me. He was living with my father, but that was becoming an impossible situation because of Dad's declining health. I needed three bedrooms, one for an office, so I could get back to the project I had left on pause.

My friends, Irv and Kathy—who increasingly felt like family to Darrell and me—encouraged me when I bid on a foreclosure, offering to help. Extravagant love it was. I was so grateful. Again I was overwhelmed with the generosity of my friends. I had so many best ones. When the bidding closed, I received the notification that I had won. I was stunned and relieved. I had a place to go. A place to heal. A place to begin again. Now, I could return to the beach and tackle the next challenge: Dad.

Walking into Dad's apartment was eye-opening. I hadn't noticed how dreadful the circumstances Jeffrey and Dad were in while Darrell was sick. I had been too preoccupied and suddenly felt neglectful of my son for allowing him to be in such a situation. Dad repeatedly had delusions because of infections making inroads into his brain. He was physically weakening, struggling to walk and falling often. I tried to get him to agree to move into a nursing home. He refused. He couldn't be without his dog, which he was incapable of properly caring for anymore. So, besides having to clean up Dad's mishaps, there were the dog's messes.

Then Dad broke his hip and had to have surgery. I thought this was his gateway to a nursing home, but after a stay in physical therapy, he seemed to improve. It didn't last. Jeffrey and I had to start using a wheelchair to move Dad around, even at his house. The idea of transitioning to a long-term care facility turned into a long battle. Dad amassed a gaggle of cohort-neighbor defenders who frequently advantaged him for his money and alcohol. One of them offered to be his caretaker. It was a shaky solution for this new nightmare that tore at my memories of Dad's past refinement. I accepted her help for one reason: I needed to buy time to move. So, I agreed and paid this amateur nurse.

The next month was a whirlwind of coordinated moves after closing on my condo. I first had to do a partial renovation of the space. Sarah and I painted, cleaned, and repaired the damage to the walls. We even placed flooring in the attic for additional storage. I began the first of five moves by removing all the trash-worthy remnants of furniture, clothing, and junk left by the previous tenant of my new home.

Simultaneously, I gained an answer to the nagging problem of Dad. He had fallen again. After taking him to the emergency room, the doctors released him to my care, even though I pleaded for them to take him to a nursing home. When the nurse couldn't get him back in my car after he had passed out and dropped to the asphalt, they admitted Dad to the hospital. They wanted to discharge him, again to me, securing an ambulance to take him home. "So, you are going to drop off an elderly man at his apartment who can't walk, wheel himself around, use the toilet, or feed himself?" I said, alarmed at the impossible demand this would put on me. Suddenly, a bed in a long-term nursing facility became available.

That started the next move—packing and moving Dad—but only after Jeffrey and I had to rip out the carpeting in a deal with the landlord to get the security deposit returned. Once a wealthy man with extravagant material luxuries, Dad was reduced to a few boxes. Discarding his belongings felt like negating his life. Mine too, in a way, for in those boxes was my real Dad, the better part of him—the polished, accomplished Dad I was proud to call mine. I went through every single item he owned, deciding which keepsakes would find a place in my home and those about to find their way to the Salvation Army or into a dumpster. When one of the neighbors asked why I was dumping a perfectly good recliner, I just held my nose, remembering the misadventures that occurred while Dad sat in it. It was heaved into the dumpster.

The moving continued, weeks turned into months. It was a montage of parts: moving out of Bill's and Nancy's where we spent the five months of Darrell's cancer battle, moving by U-Haul from our mountain home to the beach, hiring a moving company to transport my belongings from storage, as well as what was left at Dad's apartment.

The movers were the worst. Besides having to help them unload the storage unit and also load the truck with our belongings, they sheared off the towering boxes so that an entire twelve-foot-high section crashed to the ground, destroying a load of dishes and pottery. They dropped Darrell's barrister bookcase, damaging the wood and hinges. They dropped a lateral file cabinet spilling decades of paperwork and documents to the ground. They broke off the legs of Darrell's custom-made chest as it was dragged across the asphalt. Sarah had to rush to the piano with a dolly as we watched its legs ping along the ground, nearly suffering the same fate as the chest.

Their lack of care felt personally assaulting. Those material things animated parts of the past I was still clinging to.

When I found the lead mover to complain, I was at my wit's end. When our eyes met, he jumped out of the cab of the truck, where he was resting. He sauntered toward me, lifting his shirt in an excuse, "Look," he said. I got a box burn on my belly button. It really hurts." What the heck! "We're all hurting here. I need you to work. I need you to protect our things," I grumbled.

While moving out of Bill's and Nancy's, I was sorting Darrell's clothing and had the wild idea to make quilts for each of my children from his shirts. So instead of boxing his clothing, I added another project to my zany life. I cut up his shirts. I used Nancy's sewing machine to make four quilts: one for me and one for each of my children's homes. While I was sewing, I made a slipcover for the sofa and linen draperies for the new dining room. I was on overdrive and certainly living on adrenaline. I still, however, felt sane. There was also this motivation to put my life together quickly. I needed rest and space to reorient and hopefully start writing again to finish my projects. I was worried about losing momentum and the confidence of others waiting for me. I felt it.

I had traveled to the UK in February 2019 two months before Darrell had died to pitch my TV series. I was gone for three days. After a successful meeting, my attorney said, "You must be thrilled." I couldn't say. My husband was home fighting for his life. I felt like I had done well in the meeting and could be creative enough to imagine some of the recommendations given to me by the producer. I even had fun contemplating the changes to my pilot episode and proposal to accommodate the financially expedient suggestions needed by the production company.

I could feel my passion as I spoke to the company's CEO, but mostly, all I could think about at the time was getting back home. It was a curious experience to tap the resident passion for the Penn project while at the same time carrying a massive burden. I marveled at that juxtaposition. Being present to our work, however, was just what Darrell had wanted when he sent me to London. I did it. I was eager to resume that project, but it had to wait longer as my overstuffed life rolled out. Once Jeffrey and I had settled into our new home, I noticed that he wasn't sleeping. Finally, he spilled the abusive acts committed against him while in Dad's home. I was devastated. I took some blame for being too preoccupied. Jeffrey had been admitted to a psychiatric unit for a week. I didn't know all the whys. It turned out that he had been kicked out of Dad's house by his domineering fake nurse. Then I hear the worst. Jeffrey had been drugged and abused by a neighbor. He needed healing now. He needed me. We started a forever game of gin rummy since I could always get him to play cards, even during the most difficult times in his life. More than ever, his brain needed to jump the tracks of the abuse. He soon began sleeping and returned to his witty self as he began to feel safe.

Jeffrey and I started sorting the boxes in the garage. We discovered vermin had been setting up permanent housing while our things were in storage. It forced me to unpack everything so I could file a claim with the insurance company. Putting my hands on every item was a pitiless endeavor. Every damaged possession had a story. I was trashing them because of an invading creature's mutilation and/or excrement. It was insulting. Yet, I didn't have a choice. Just when I'd relive one memory, I'd be struck by another. I'd pick up a photo of us and feel Darrell's off-screen kisses. I could hear him play with our children after unpacking beach gear. My brain slowed to a crawl reliving our life and straining to make decisions.

I diverged from urgent tasks a few times to have mini break-downs. I couldn't squirm out of my skin fast enough. I drove just to be alone. I didn't want my children or friends to see me shedding my modus operandi, not because I was embarrassed, but because I didn't exactly know what was happening or who I might become. I wanted the pain. It was a grim endorsement of my life as I morphed into someone I didn't yet know or trust. I found myself just driving without a destination when I couldn't be around people. I wound up at the beach often, just sitting inside my car, not even remembering the drive there. Somehow in my car, I could be me.

Fall came and I needed to start working with a writer from the UK who I had hired to help me package my project for the pro-duction company. She decided it was best for her, after I postponed our start date, to begin after the first of the year. Frankly, it was a relief. My grief might as well have been Punxsutawney Phil seeing his shadow, predicting a longer winter. I needed more time since I was playing whack-a-mole with my pain and increasing confusion, anyway.

Our first Christmas was surprisingly sweet and meaningful for my family. Brian and Margarita were the perfect hosts for our holiday. My children loved their quilts. The anticipation of being without Darrell in the weeks ahead of the holidays was worse than the actual day. Gratitude filled the air around us. We all sighed with relief when the day was done. January came, and I was so glad I had set up my space to work. I felt at home, surrounded by my books. I needed a lot of focus to get back into the seventeenth century and be able to stay there. That was going to be a challenge, but I wanted it.

> My grief might as well have been Punxsutawney
> Phil seeing his shadow, predicting a longer winter. I
> needed more time since I was playing whack-a-mole
> with my pain... .

It was time for a board meeting for my non-profit. It was rough since it was the first since Darrell died. I needed clarity on moving forward without him. Besides, we had decisions to make about funding since the money raised from the gala event was nearly gone after my travels to the UK, my salary, and the payments for professional fees. I told my board members about my plans with my writer, Alison. I assumed that I would be finished with her in a few months. She and I planned on meeting up in the States for a long weekend or even a week. That would have been perfect and something I knew would be life-giving. I had already sent her the best of my work. I had a sixty-page, six-column organized timeline for her to grab hold of the context. She had my pilot episode and my version of the story map. She was to tidy it up. That board meeting left me encouraged and a bit more focused.

Then a friend passed away in New York. When I returned home from the funeral, I wasn't feeling well. Suddenly I had fevers in the 103-to-104-degree range for weeks. The fevers continued near 100 degrees for an entire month. I began coughing. Soon, I had trouble breathing. My doctor now believed I had COVID but no one was testing for it then, though it was known and becoming an epidemic in New York City. The severity of the illness continued for months.

After the first month of fevers, I started Skyping with Alison, even though I couldn't speak one complete sentence without coughing. COVID was shutting down travel everywhere, so even if I hadn't been ill, we had to meet online. In any event, it was the best fun I had had since Darrell passed away. I felt alive even though Alison said to me once, "Lorrie just let me talk and you nod." My coughing fits were disquieting for both of us. Yet, reflexive knowledge flowed out of me as if I had it all curated as soon as she needed it.

I knew the history as well as knew how to tell the story. I knew what pieces would set up, escalate, and pay off the story. I knew the turning points. I knew many of my characters well enough to know what they'd do when the history wasn't explicit. I knew what I wanted the audience to experience. I knew what it was all about and how every piece of context had to serve that specific purpose. Alison was a point of light for my confidence. I didn't know if I could re-engage, but she pulled my gifts out of me. It gave me hope that my work could meet a need in the world while at the same time giving me joy. I felt it.

The first year of widowhood had nearly come to an end when I wrote in my journal all I had learned about life and myself. I wrote to Darrell:

My love, I learned these curious things this year:
- That my habitual be-it-unto-me defiance of hellishness wasn't a wise stance.
- That moving for five straight months is HELL. You always said moving was going to be hell's perpetual job description. I think so too.

- That a drill can replace a key and a locksmith when trying to get into your treasures.
- That your little tenet about gratitude being the key to everything is true until it's not.
- That I am horribly alone without you despite our children.
- That my kids are saviors in their own right.
- That if I don't find alone time, I am doomed to confusion.
- That if I don't find a connection with people, I am just doomed.
- That you were right to repent at the end of your life for having too much stuff.
- That we have too much stuff.
- That I could lose sentimentality over possessions.
- That memories aren't enough.
- That I am easily taken off my game.
- That our dream keeps me alive.
- That crooked things can drive me crazy. Who knew, I'd end up like you.
- That I have the best friends.
- That the only thing that matters is the minutes right in front of me.
- That platitudes and hypotheticals are a waste of time and words.
- That I can be frightened into a panic.
- That I can be embarrassed by my weakness. I need to think about that one.
- That I am not invincible but brave.
- That I am proud of myself.

I had made it past a milestone I thought intact but acutely aware of all my shapeshifting. I understood what psychological injury can do from being in persistent turmoil.[8] I also was aware of how chaos can be a frenemy, doling out trouble to excuse inner healing and change. It not always easy to see especially when our souls and bodies get inured to trouble. I realized that after Darrell and I had first married, and I had withdrawal symptoms from the chaos of the life and death I had been in while Jeffrey and I were recovering (Chapter 3).

As a new bride, I had found myself feeling restless completing ordinary tasks. Yet, ordinary was exactly what allowed me to heal. Now it was true again.[9] I was looking forward to entering the sanctuary of the ordinary. I was going to embrace it deliberately this time; I knew I was teetering emotionally. Plus, I hadn't even begun to think about my sister's passing. I just couldn't afford give in to it any of it just yet. I had one more difficult life event ahead and that was Dad's upcoming death. I didn't have a choice.

---

8   "An emotional trauma may induce a cascade of neurobiological events that have long-lasting consequences even altered gene expression." Giotakos, Neurobiology of Emotional Trauma, *Psychiayriki*, Vol. 31, 2 (2020) 162-171.

9   Good-Grief.org: https://good-grief.org/wp-content/uploads/2017/04/How-To-Create-a-Safe-Space-for-Someone-Who-is-Grieving.pdf

DAD, DEATH,
DISCONNECTING

"How's the writing coming?" someone texted me early in May 2020 while I was with Dad. I typed back, "Um, it's not. I am at a nursing home watching my father die." But, this person knew that. I erased the text before sending it. It felt snarky and I didn't want to be. Their message wasn't completely from deep space, however. I had received a letter a couple of weeks prior, on my wedding anniversary of April 21st, stating that I was losing my funding for not producing enough for the nonprofit in the year after Darrell's death (I mentioned this in Chapter one). Despite my initial knee-jerk reaction, I truly thought the whole argument was a fluke. I had little patience for analysis. Dad was barely alive.

I was allowed to see Dad in his last hours. His nurses defied protocol to let me in the facility amid COVID restrictions. They even overlooked my coughing, a leftover symptom from my having the virus earlier that year. Day and night for a week I sat with Dad, trying to help him pass peacefully. I played all his favorite songs. I called my brothers and held the phone for Dad as he feebly expressed his love and said his goodbyes. But, Dad still wasn't dead, even after eight days of no fluids. I wondered how that was possible.

Dad had a lot of anger toward his own father; I pondered if this unresolved issue was the reason he was still hanging on. When he could still talk, I asked him if he could forgive his father. He shook his head. I tried to persuade him. "We have been forgiven so much in our lives. Right, Dad?" I knew that he knew exactly what I was talking about since his skeletons had fallen out of the closet more than once. But he just wouldn't forgive. I understood. What his father, Millard, had done was unforgivable, including the abandonment my dad was forced to live with.

Once, in my twenties, Darrell and I were alone with Dad on his dock in Hawaii Kai, Honolulu. We were asking about his father. As Dad recalled his story, he stopped with a raised fist toward the heavens to declare with guttural certainty that he would never forgive his father. The visceral reaction I had to his judgment made the hair stand up on my arms. I worried at the time how those inner vows and judgments Dad had been carrying all his life might backfire, as inner vows and judgments do, even if Dad didn't reflect on his experience in those terms. Darrell saw it too. He whispered in my ear with eerie foretelling, "Ken's gonna die just like his Dad—alone and broke." I couldn't imagine it, especially the *broke* part.

Sure enough, Dad was dying just as his father had and would have been alone had I not been there. Part of me was intentional about breaking a pattern of generational mindsets. Tending to Dad was with that awareness, not just to work out my grief, but for my own legacy. The forgiveness was not merely for Dad: it was for me and my family. I believed releasing my father from any obligation for his failings could pave the way for my children and grandchildren to be free of hereditary iniquities. I had seen many times when counseling others how unforgiveness manifests in destructive family patterns. I also saw how familial weaknesses can be traced to previous generations whether the family realized it or not.

Dad had spent his life trying to prove that he was never going to end up like his father. It was a driving motivation that pushed my father to great heights of success, tinged as it were with a bit of narcissism. But, his bitterness toward his father masked his childhood wounding and kept him from the growth that could have come with serious reflection. Self-made men, like Dad, are at this risk if their personal value is in what they create rather than in their being. When what they create (including the image of themselves) fails them in any way, it is deeply personal. The complexities and ambiguities of life's pilgrimage are lost on them. Now that Dad had lost his former glory, he spent his elder years drinking every day and reliving past successes and felt betrayals. They came out of his mouth incessantly. The thing that he couldn't confess was responsibility for any of his imperfections. I knew he felt them though. There were occasional times I had said, "But Dad, what about..." His eyes would dart before he'd look me straight in the eyes... and then say nothing for lingering moments. Suddenly, he'd change the subject. Every time. I felt sad for him.

Finally, the day came for Dad to leave his body. My phone battery had worn down, so I could no longer repeat-play his favorite faith song, "On the Wings of a Dove". I had hoped he'd like to float away with that tune. I started singing the song to him whenever it seemed he was breathing his last. But he just kept breathing. Finally, I turned on the television. Ironically, the movie *Mummy* played on the only channel I could find. It matched my scenario. The creepiness was nearly humorous.

Ultimately, an image of Dad entered my mind. I turned off the television. I saw Dad at eight years old curled up in a corner, cowering as his father's rage and abuse flared. Compassion flooded my soul. I realized how difficult it had been for him to let go of his hurt. Filled with compassion, I decided I would forgive his father for him, not fully knowing if it was a role I could play. I did it, anyway. His torment over his father was the only thing I could think of that might be causing him such a struggle. As Dad lay there unconscious, I spoke to him. I addressed the stunted child in his soul, reasoning that his spirit was fully aware. I hoped.

"Dad, I know what Millard did to you is unforgivable. It was cruel of him to beat you when you tried to protect your mom. It was unfair to make you think you had to be strong. It was unfair to make you have to provide for the family when he left. It was too much, Dad, for anyone, especially for you as a young boy. But, Dad, he couldn't love or maybe he didn't know he could be free enough to love."

Through tears streaming down my face I continued, "So, Dad... I forgive Millard for you. You don't need his love to be whole and free. I love you, Dad. God does too. He loves you more than any father could."

> I had long forgiven my father for his emotional
> absence, but the little girl in me still wanted her dad.
> I tried to stretch the good memories I had from my
> younger years into a lifetime of them but never could.

Dad's eyes flickered. I thought it might be a response to my appeal, but I didn't know. His zombielike appearance made it hard to tell. What I did know was that a quick minute later, I watched Dad's arms and hands curl into his chest like a dying spider. I wanted to look away. I spun on my feet, raising my hands to the top of my head before I bolstered myself. I grabbed Dad's rigid arms and pulled him to me. I held his bony figure in an awkward embrace; then Dad let out a long, final exhale. It frightened me. I hastily let go. He flopped back into the bed as three nurses arrived, while I spontaneously yelped, "Jesus!" I hoped they didn't see me drop my poor dad's corpse. All three female nurses were teary-eyed as they entered the room (Dad was a charmer).

I had long forgiven my father for his emotional absence, but the little girl in me still wanted her dad. I tried to stretch the good memories I had from my younger years into a lifetime of them but never could. I remembered the fishing trips, the foot-long Dodger dogs at Dodger's games in Los Angeles, boating in his speed boat and cabin cruiser, the water skiing, the camping, and Sunday barbecues at his bay-side home in East Honolulu. Still, decades of his insobriety hacked family memories. It was a different kind of grief from that for my husbands, who both left me without the snag of regret. This grief was delivered by the sadness of concluded hope for deep engagement. I felt like the seventy-year-old man at Darrell's funeral who commented after hearing Darrell's blessings to our children. With glistening eyes, the man said, "If only my father had spoken words like that to me." Like my older friend, I will never hear the specific words of affirmation every child's heart needs to hear, no matter what age.

I hosted a Zoom funeral in May. It was a wonder that I could since I was still coughing from COVID-19. Yet, I managed to tell the story of forgiveness from my time with Dad before he died. The theme of forgiveness saturated the call. All three of my brothers' (Dan, Kevin, and Josh) words were moving. We were able to square Dad's rascally side with his humanity. There was a clear sense of the common struggle to do our best with the life we are given, trying to live up to our ideals, while also knowing the ease with which we can fall short. Life events stunted Dad, particularly because they occurred when he was a child.[10]

Dad was like a lobster with one overdeveloped claw juxtaposed with its smaller contracted one. To achieve what he had in business was his big claw, even as the other claw shrank on the basics. The Zoom funeral became a necessary intimate and healing time. It gave everyone permission to feel their pain and disappointment (none of which needed elaboration in this knowing group), yet from a place of compassion for Dad's struggles. Gratitude poured out for his good qualities, particularly his generosity and work ethic. We owned Dad's infrequently spoken but true words of love for his family.

My friends and former pastors when we lived in Hawaii, Sam and Nancy, also attended the funeral. They knew my family inti-

---

10   "Early abuse and neglect can deregulate the child's developing neurobiological system..." Clair Le Dorze, et al. "Emotional remodeling with oxytocin durably rescues trauma-induced behavioral and neuro-morphological changes in rats: a promising treatment for PTSD." *Translational psychiatry* 10.1 (2020): 1-13.

mately. They called later to tell me what a miracle they had witnessed… and it truly was. Remnants of bitterness vanished in the loving space we created to honor a man we all loved despite his shortcomings and in spite of his gambling away the family's fortunes in his later years. As this occurred, I was not functioning well in my private life. I knew I was tired, but it was more than that. By the time of Dad's funeral in May, I started experiencing glitches in my thought processes.

Stuck phrases and aborted thoughts bothered me, particularly because this had not been the case in the previous months when I felt competent to do the tasks in front of me. I managed to tend to Dad, secure his long-term care, move "everyone," and unpack thirty-five years of my life and eighty of Dad's. I purchased and renovated my home, sewed memory quilts and draperies, and even painted artwork for over my bed. I traveled, worked, collaborated, wrote, and recovered from my illness (sort of, I was still going to cough for another year). I was creative, productive, and often inspired. But I was changing, morphing into a person I didn't recognize.

My primary care physician came into my life in a more active way to help me sort out this new cognitive malfunctioning. "You are strong, Lorrie, but not Wonder Woman," Dr. Joy nearly scolded. "Trauma is cumulative, my dear. Losing your funding at the same time as your dad's death pushed you too far. Then, she gave me a word picture, "I see that you built this beautiful ship with your husband, and now it may crash against the rocks. You are holding the rope to steady it, wondering if help is coming. But it's not coming. I am telling you, for right now, you have to let it go before it drags you under. My job is to keep you alive!" I nearly sobbed on the other end of the phone, not because it could be foretelling about my work, but because she had captured my journey. Nonetheless, I couldn't let go. It seemed my life depended on saving this ship—it was my future.

> "You are strong, Lorrie, but not Wonder Woman," Dr.
> Joy nearly scolded. "Trauma is cumulative, my dear."

Dr. Joy kept checking in on me. One day I asked her if she could write a letter, explaining the duress I was under. I wanted help to buy the time I needed and thought folks would listen and understand better if a professional validated my state of mind and see that I had done all that was humanly possible during some impossible circumstances to set up my life to steer the ship. I was panicking.

"Let's talk about that, Lorrie," she replied, leading me into the green grass of enlightenment. "Okay, so here's how it goes. I begin to summarize your life events, which should have shown physiological effects sooner, by the way. I review your life by saying in the last year your sister died, then your husband, and your dad, and that would be enough, but then you... blah, blah, blah (she gives a montage of events). On top of that, you were sick for two months, and your lungs are still not back to normal. You are not well; you show signs of real injury, and you have a d—n good reason for it." (She could talk to me that way, using a few perfectly-placed expletives for emphasis.)

As soon as Dr. Joy rattled off the list of life events, I instantly heard with new ears how trying to explain was not going to help. "AH! So, that will only prove the arguments against me." I fully comprehended. She went on to warn me that a letter from her would make things worse since producing was the point. What was even more clarifying, however, was how desperate the situation made me feel. I couldn't factor in the sudden insecurity I felt. I only knew I must contain my attempts to be understood and try to find solid ground. My mind reeled. I had just wanted a bit more time to regroup.

The truth was, I could produce under very difficult circumstances. That some couldn't see it boggled my mind. I had been communicating during this time with many donors about my progress. I wrote them a note of gratitude once, inspired by a page that randomly fell out of a worn Bible that said, "I thank God upon every remembrance of you." They had been the wind behind me so many times. I shared how I now found myself surprised by joy when working with my writer in the UK. I shared how I had clarity on how the next year would play out by being occupied by Darrell and William Penn.

It created standing room for me. I assumed that I might be walking into that figurative bright meadow I imagined while in Knott Wood in England. I believed that I could finally process my life with Darrell and also have the dedicated time for Penn, which would give my brain two important jobs with these two important men. I was grateful for the extraordinary agility that kept me from a crumbling edge I imagined was just there.

Now I would neither be welcoming grief when it decided to poke out its head... nor would I be working. What was I to do? Was I merely living to justify my existence to people who no longer believed in me? I knew better too. In the past, I taught relationship theory that said there is no truth or explanation equal to the task of displacing root-bound opinions or judgments. Yet here I was writhing, feeling foolish, and embarrassing myself trying to explain. I sniveled my way into the muck of talking too much. I remembered my husband. Darrell was best at abiding by the principle of knowing what environment was necessary to be heard. Often he would say, "Know your audience," understanding the need to move along and not allow people to form further judgments. It also could help them by not giving a landing place for negativity, by allowing their words to boomerang back to them for reflection (if possible). In a weird way it helped me to finally believe my explaining wasn't helping anyone. I wondered what Darrell would have done because I know he would have been flabbergasted and at least sympathized with me. It was he who told me of promises made before his death that I would be able to continue our work.

To be fair, so many people had invested in our work, and it was reasonable to have expectations. I, too, felt the pressure to get to market with my work. Now, I just needed a real minute. I saw my two choices and didn't know how to prioritize them. On the one hand, I needed to perform. I wanted to. On the other hand were my health issues and this new and sudden phenomenon, where I noticed myself flipping easily from engagement to real detachment.

Dr. Joy prescribed an antidepressant. "I am not depressed, I told her." She smiled knowingly. "Trauma and depression have cross-over symptoms, Lorrie." To convince me I was reasonably injured, she insisted I take a stress test to convince me to "let go of the rope." I could not comprehend how I went from feeling safe to feeling so threatened within a month. I ordered a book she recommended, *The Anxiety and Phobia Workbook*.[11] She warned, "You're going to score high on the life events test in that book, just saying."

---

11   Edmund J. Bourne, PhD, *The Anxiety & Phobia Workbook*, sixth edition, New Harbinger Publications, Oakland, CA. 2015

The test had a range of scores. If a person's score was between 150 and 300, they might be suffering from chronic stress. If the score was over 300, it was likely the person was experiencing detrimental effects of cumulative stress.[12] My life-events score totaled 690. I told Dr. Joy that I had scored 600 instead. I don't know why I had left off the additional 90, as if the extra number would flag me for an asylum faster than a 600 score would. Maybe I thought she'd think I had exaggerated. But she didn't flinch. "See!" she exclaimed, giving me the courage to look again into her worried but accepting eyes.

At least I didn't have any of the listed phobias in the book—not ones I could recognize. In any event, this was a wake-up call. I had to let go or I might delay going forward or worse. I dutifully took the medicine she prescribed, although brisk walks and meaningful time with friends seemed to have more of an immediate effect. I could never tell if the medicine ever did remedy my mood.

I continued to worry over the loss of momentum and support, but that concern slowly became secondary as the world I had counted on fractured into pieces. The stakes were clearer. There would be no "snapping out of it," as I had been urged to do by well-meaning folks whose back-handed analyses weighed on my mind.

I thanked God for Dr. Joy helping me to see the risk factors, including the possibility of developing a complicated grief disorder from the accumulation of life stressors that made grief work impossible.[13] Finally, my body made me believe her. It wasn't an easy

---

12   Ibid, p. 46.
13   Mayo Clinic, Complicated Grief, 1998-2022 Mayo Foundation for Medical Education and Research (MFMER). Web access 07/23/2021, www.mayoclinic.com).

pivot. I started to feel precariously vulnerable giving in to weaknesses that I didn't understand and went against my dogma.

The ideas that helped me through many difficult days in the past were: we don't know the end of our strength and we are stronger than we think; we don't need circumstances to change but only to become braver; obstacles are merely challenges that lead to good changes and are learning opportunities; weakness can actually be strength because it positions us to receive something new... but, most importantly, it deals a death blow to an egotism that tempts us to be over and above others; failures don't exist when they are events that merely teach us what doesn't work.

One of the popular messages I had spoken in public meetings was called "So What?" Its theme was about dispelling the lie that failure or setbacks are accusatory or defining. I believed it, truly. I still do. It is how people perceive an event or an accusation, whether it becomes stoppable. I suddenly needed to add nuance because I was reacting like my weakness meant something: I was stoppable. I wrote in my journal in February 2021about the confusing opposites in my life. "Funny thing, I do trust my capacity in one hand as surely as I fear my incapacity in the other." As was a habit, I also wrote to Darrell in my journal that month that he would have been proud of me after I spoke at a public meeting. I told him what the young man said: "I don't like history but I can listen to you all day." And the woman who said, "What I like about you is that you can back up what you say." Then, I immediately told him how I cried nearly all the way home from that meeting, wanting to hide. Coincidentally enough, I was writing the journal entry recalling the successful speaking engagement but also my feelings of failure and disorganization, Jeff came into my room waving a credit card.

"Where did you get that," I asked. "You just gave it to me Mom, like ten minutes ago." Sarah blurted out another time, "Mom, your memory." These were no longer "so-whats" but scary glitches. My previous mantras worked until they didn't. They didn't.

I shuddered quietly watching evidence pile up for those who perhaps needed a way out of the nonprofit that funded my life and work. I gave it to them, even while hearing that it was believed Darrell had died because he somehow had lived in fear and therefore had sinned. I said nothing in rebuttal. My oldest, Jeffrey, having struggled with a traumatic brain injury his whole life, was also in the room when these words were spoken. He stood up suddenly when he heard that negative verdict about his dad and reproved, "You don't know. If that were true, I would have been dead long ago." His defense of me and his dad was pure love, though it did not change any minds. Nor did I want it to.

> A nuanced shift in my belief structure began. I saw that it wasn't gallant to keep my two dukes up all the time.

I merely cowered. It felt like I was Neo right before his mouth was stitched shut in the movie, *Matrix,* asking for my phone. My circumstances were saying, as Agent Smith did, "What good is a phone call when you can't speak." I finally comprehended my audience as Darrell would have warned me long before. I became quiet.

A nuanced shift in my belief structure began. I saw that it wasn't gallant to keep my two dukes up all the time. My ideas on strength weren't as consistent as I had thought, if I wanted to live true and were brave enough to go into the untethered state of mind that allowed me to change. The problem became trust. If I am found wanting, could I trust that all will be well (eventually)? I thought of that line from the movie, *The Best Exotic Marigold Hotel*, when the hotel manager comforts a guest, "Everything will be all right in the end. If it's not all right, it is not yet the end." I scoffed at that well-wishing at first because well-wishing is no guarantee. What makes things "all right" and equal to the task of facing unbearable losses is peace, not outcomes. I needed peace. The kind that comes from knowing that nothing is so broken that I could be robbed of hope. It seemed an impossible transition juxtaposed to more loss.

I wondered if I had to say goodbye really and forever to a dream or to important relationships and past securities. My mouth was stitched shut. I could no longer speak to the words coming at me. "See, we knew she couldn't write." They were ironically true words now anyway. I relinquished with a shrug, knowing I couldn't write or produce. My mind could not form the connections needed to be creative. When this trouble finally drilled down to the core of me, I saw that my panic over losing my funding was because the Penn dream felt like my last connection to Darrell, and he was being ripped out of my arms once again. The pain of that was jarring. I was emptied by the loss of promise, the loss of who I was, and the wonder of who I was to become.

I began to block communications because some of them forced me into a song and dance while I was drowning. "A life vest would have helped," I later tried to joke with Dr. Joy while retelling my seemingly irresponsible avoidances. She didn't laugh; she nodded vigorously. When I told her what I had done to block calls and not open emails, I thought she would have a remedy for what I deemed as a possible dysfunction; instead, she was proud of me. She reminded me that I was in survival mode and there was a need to limit the noise that was toxic to me.

She was a godsend, making me feel confident enough to make decisions for my health. I needed to be true to myself. I needed to move at my own pace and with my own revelation. I needed to live in real time, with a real body that needed tending and practical help. Some of those I had counted on could not go with me now. All I knew was that it was right for me to go on an undisclosed solo journey now.

In the movie, *Land*, actress Robin Wright told her counselor who questioned her about why she didn't want to share her grief journey with others. Robin said it was difficult to be around people who just wanted her "to be better." She continued, "I did [want to talk] and then I realized why would I want to share... they can't [share] anyway." These lines in that script were written by someone in the know.

When there was finally nothing more to talk about regarding my work or my inner struggle in the middle of 2020, a water leak sprang in my kitchen. At first, I tried to find and fix the water problem myself, breaking down in tears from the struggle of ripping out moldy cabinets. I hired a contractor, but after three months of delays, I fired him. I had to finish the project myself, but now the entire kitchen was torn apart. I learned to use Darrell's power tools. I built and hung cabinets. I even moved electrical boxes (getting a jolt only two hair-raising times). I lived in a disaster zone for six months, doing dishes outside and in the bathroom. For some inexplicable reason, the project was a welcome relief. The physical energy outpaced my emotional energy and granted me a pardon.

Darrell and my Penn project were again across a chasm, although at times, I would jump the divide and feel every bit of their loss. I suddenly understood why people become reckless after emotional trauma because exerting myself physically in doing this work somehow connected me to me.

By Christmas the kitchen was finished. My kids instinctively gave me a change of pace and scenery. They took me to Charleston, South Carolina for a holiday. It was perfect. We made new memories. We had genuine interaction and plenty of new culinary adventures… and it brought me back to my neglected inner pain. In the next months, the early half of 2021, I came to hard terms with my situation. I might have gone there sooner or later, no matter what the catalyst would have been. I had been pushed to my edges many times that first year, but I hadn't felt endangered… or that it was an anomaly. Now time was against me as a loss of momentum opened doors to the Black Riders (the Nazgul), who in J.R.R. Tolkien's *Fellowship Of The Ring* were continuously able to unsettle the Hobbit's Shire that had been the depiction of happiness and peace. In this new experience, my go-to defiance of taunting troubles was in the past—and no booster for my ego could help.

I learned that my shire could be terrorized, repeatedly. In less acute times, these types of trials hadn't robbed my strength. Now, honest doubt prevailed. Part of me was curious to discover any upshot' but, at first, I was too focused on the evil circling me to tap into that imaginative side of me. It showed too. I was easily overwhelmed and distracted. Following a thought or simple task through was now laborious and often impossible. Longer periods of disassociation swept over me. It was hard to distinguish between relevant and irrelevant information.

I spent hours content to stare off into nothingness. It was a curiosity as much as it was unsettling. In the middle of this behavior, I also thought of the disengaged folks I had misunderstood for exactly this same condition. I thought of those folks I'd occasionally find on a sidewalk, talking to themselves or someone in their head. Suddenly, I had a new compassion while staring and sitting alone, surprisingly content to do so. I reminisced. My mind visited the five months of caring for Darrell and all I had done, to no avail, to save him. I remembered his faith and positive attitude while sick. I had little of that. I felt so removed from the optimism I had always known. I traveled through my memories without a sense of shame for where I was. I felt abandoned to it. That was good... it seemed.

> For the very first time, I realized that I wasn't going to resist what life was going to show me through this next phase. More critically, I realized that I shouldn't. It was my new goal.

In that quiet place, it must have been how I was lured into the river, where I would begin that float (mentioned in the introduction), where noises above the water's surface would be muffled... because they were. At first, I hesitated letting myself remain motionless and letting threats stay on shore. I thought I needed to know how long this journey would take and where I would end up, still grasping for comprehension, still grasping for trust, still fearing more betrayal or misapprehension of others, even with my children. But I needed the quiet... to let go of the outcomes I had wanted, could project, or could explain.

Once in a while, I would hit the rocky shallows of bewilderment. It felt a bit unfair that after the sum of my life to this point, I had more uncertainty to face as the third year of widowhood was looming. It was far from any triumphal ending to my time of grief. I wasn't even getting ordinary anytime soon. More and more, I was able to recognize false hopes and mistaken beliefs in the coming silence. The self, which by definition is so full of itself, was bowing to a goodness that comes in rest... and perhaps only does so once the striving stops. When I could do it though, it brought me back into smoother, deeper waters.

For the very first time, I realized that I wasn't going to resist what life was going to show me through this next phase. More critically, I realized that I shouldn't. It was my new goal.

RECONNECTING

"Hey Mom, get back in the shower!" squawked my daughter, Sarah, at me one day as I descended downstairs in my robe.

"What?" I responded.

"That wasn't long enough," she declared. There was a pause before she continued.

"Ever hear of self-care?"

"Pfft," I huffed back as I squeezed my brows, being faintly humored by her attempt to moderate my bathing habits.

"I can't think of anything more to do in there," I replied in jest while pondering what she needed to see in me. The shower wasn't the problem but her alarm over neglected details she supposed. When I was working so hard that first year and spending every extra minute on the Penn project, she had pasted a Post-it note on my desktop computer. It merely read, "Work Life Balance."

Sarah has always been instinctive and saw that I was pushing too hard and not allowing myself any priority. She theorized about it—out loud. Was it my generational mindset? Was it that I was so used to being the giver such that I couldn't receive? Was it my upbringing? Was it the church culture that bolstered the practice of sacrifice? She questioned it all. Yet, she, too, worked extraordinarily hard. She was with me during all of it. She organized her friends to help with all the logistics of moving that first year. Those friends, Loren, Tony, Jasmine, Liz, and more became my kids too. They forfeited their time, their bodies, and their money in loving and practical support. We experienced meaningful moments—heart-wrenching and life-infusing interactions. It was pure love, deprived of the shade of self-regard.

Yet I was behaving oddly to those around me. The truth was, I didn't recognize myself either, even though I knew I was repeatedly and sufficiently washed from my bath times. Almost. There was this one curious time noted by Jeffrey. One evening, he delicately asked if he could run an Epsom salt bath for me. Suddenly, his question startled me into another reality. "Okay, Jeff," I obliged, getting up from Darrell's recliner—the recliner he had lived in the last few months of his life. It was the recliner that became the five-square feet of space I could escape to when it seemed that the sky was falling. I walked into the bathroom to see a lit candle and a glass of water next to the filling tub.

The dissociation I was experiencing was my brain's way of protecting me. It was my body doing its job to keep me stable. I didn't fully grasp how I could lose chunks of time, but I did see my capacity hit a threshold. Distraction worked for a time and was an important strategy, but now my brain and emotions needed wandering time to integrate my new life in a safe place.

I needed to limit those who couldn't accept the pace I was able to process my life and suffering... not just over Darrell's death but the layers of losses I experienced. The only thing I knew was that it was going to be prolonged; it didn't bother me at face value. What did bother me was wondering whether detachment would become a permanent feature of my personality. I felt pressure and the need to shake it off... somehow.

Neurologist, Lisa Shulman, speaks of her trauma of losing her husband and as a scientist when she says, "We can't delay integration, processing, and awareness forever."[14] I had to take care of myself but what would self-care look like if I could do it? I knew: go home to Hawaii. It took me out of a setting that increasingly felt muddled and noxious. I also knew that my abridged state of mind was hard on my children; besides the environment was too narrowly focused on me. So, going home seemed like a good thing for all, and it put me into an environment in which the air was pure *Aloha*.

I boarded my nonstop flight to Honolulu from Newark, noticing the neutral disposition in my soul. I liked it. I didn't watch any movies, read a book, open my computer, or visit with a single soul on the flight. I merely slept—for nine hours, I slept in my gifted first-class seat. When I awoke, I was thrilled. I couldn't remember the last time I had slept so long. A sense of adventure flickered when I spotted the familiar turquoise waters and lush island vegeta-

---

14   Lisa M. Shulman, *Before and After Loss, A Neurologist's Perspective on Loss, Grief, and Our Brain.* (2019, John Hopkins University Press) Audio Book, Chapter 5

tion during the descent into Honolulu. I liked that too. The feeling was furnished with a nod of relief.

I arrived without having set plans, unsure how I might react to being in Hawaii again. I didn't contact any friends ahead of time for just that reason. The islands held happy memories, but Darrell's death threatened to hack them into bits. Or maybe not. A gut feeling steered me; it said I needed to be quiet. If I talked too much or tried to put a positive spin on my grief—an effort I often undertook to make it easier for others to be with me—I might forfeit connecting with myself. For now, I had silence and beauty to unhand me of the clumsy expectations from people, myself, or any such stage theory protocol, for which I was completely out of sync with anyway.

Both times while being widowed, I hadn't found stage theory helpful. It was confusing to measure myself by the proposed five steps of grief since I never fit neatly into those patterns and certainly never in an orderly fashion. It was as if recovery were like riding a train through its progressive stops until one reached Never Never Land. Then, you learn that those steps were originally a study of the dying (rather than a remedy for those remaining in the land of the living). They seemed to make them tactless for those of us left behind, even though the common experiences with the dying can be very insightful.

The first named stage of grief is denial, for example. It is a defensive mechanism that protects us during the shock of loss. Knowing denial is normal makes the magical thinking not so strange—like the magical thinking I just had during my travels to Honolulu. It happened when I heard a funny story and immediately thought I couldn't wait to tell Darrell, knowing he'd find it hysterical. My mind knew that he was dead; but somewhere in my brain, he wasn't. If I were to be literal about stage theory, I might have thought that I was deviant because it was now two years past the event of Darrell's death. Denial is supposed to be the first stage one progresses through.

For me and so many others, the aspects of grief over any loss are more like fluctuations that come and go as we evolve and find new meaning and identity. Grief must have this characteristic lest it be insufferable stress to manage. Some steps may never appear or do so out of the five-stage order. From my experience, they were triggered at the oddest of times. Accepting the flux of it all helped me immensely, particularly because it resonated with my instinctive approach to life, which didn't square with efforts to make people regular in an irregular world.

Still, at home, I felt the pressure to make grief palatable, knowing it was difficult for people to watch me struggle. That's why one person helped themselves to an excuse for my state of being saying, "Even the mighty fall… I guess." Even though that comment was taken as a personal rejection of my humanity, I was also sad for them. That comment wasn't merely about me. It represents a mindset intolerant of weakness and thus, in my mind, was a coping mechanism impervious to growth, not to mention love. I was attentive to that worldview even when being tempted to dissemble or find a way to justify a diminishing me. Therein lay the problem. Dealing with traumatic loss is a natural and disfiguring event, requiring a very private metamorphosis. As the process of metamorphosis takes place, the caterpillar's old body must die in the cocoon and turn into goo before it is transformed. I was goo; and as goo goes, it's not that easy to hold together.

Dealing with traumatic loss is a natural and disfiguring event, requiring a very private metamorphosis.

Nonetheless, it felt good being adorned with sweet-smelling
leis when my brother, Kevin, picked me up from the airport. He
drove me to Sam and Nancy's house, where I would be staying
for the next month. I easily fell right into their loving arms and
the busy but relaxed rhythm of Hawaiian life. They provided the
freedom I needed and the keys to their Mini Cooper, whenever I
needed it to do whatever I needed to do.

My first morning in Honolulu, I drove over the Ko'olau Mountains to Kailua Beach to see the sunrise after stopping off at a local
beachside café for my Kona coffee. I found a spot under a tree and
watched the few early morning adventures stroll along the shoreline. I felt a twinge of loneliness, quickly scuttled by resuming my
self-imposed photography job I had quit after my European travels
two years previous. I pointed my camera toward the horizon, waiting for the sun when a couple, walking hand in hand, entered the
lens. They fascinated me. Oh, that's what the world's been up to, I
thought. The woman said something to her man to make him roll
his head back and laugh before he playfully pulled her close as they
continued to stroll near the water's edge.

I imagined her sharing a secret privy only to them. I wondered
how long they'd been together. I hoped they appreciated the moment
they had just shared as much as I did. Emotions I had driven down
bubbled up. I didn't cry, but I might have had I lingered on those
thoughts. I turned my gaze to where the forever sky met the vast Pacific
Ocean. I felt small and unseen. It had been a long while since I took
up space to be intimately known as that beach couple had shown me.

Sam and Nancy left for an outer island trip during my first week. I had helped Nancy select new tile for her kitchen; when she left, I had the task of picking it up from the home improvement center. It was an unexpected distraction. I liked revisiting old stomping grounds where I surprisingly felt at home. As a former interior designer, I was happy to find inspiration for their project. When Nancy returned, she and I were in full-blown renovation mode, which had the effect of keeping me mostly quiet until a random emotion or memory would pop up.

Nancy's and Sam's listening always allowed me to dig deep inside myself, no matter what was lurking in there. Once, in my late thirties, when Darrell and I were struggling with the church we pastored in Pennsylvania, I was telling Nancy about some difficulties we were having. She told me a story about a meeting Sam was in where a pastor said he wished he'd be able to vent his frustrations in a safe environment without being judged, wishing he could just say a more accurate word to describe his feelings. I'll never forget the exact asphalt I drove on when I felt permission to do just that. Eyebrows raised, I took a breath and let out a half-hearted poo-word. Soon I was saying it properly, repeatedly, hitting the steering wheel while doing it. When I did, whatever snarl I had melted into tears and then sprouted into hilarity. Nancy joined me in this victory as her infectious, trademark laughter liberated me from the mire within. We laughed all the way home. The anomaly of it stunned her. It did me too but that was the funny part. When we stopped being amused, she merely asked, "Do you feel better now?" We laughed some more. She was the environment that doesn't judge. That coaxing of hidden feelings happened repeatedly while I was with her in Hawaii, though I was not saying the poo-word again.

In the middle of Nancy's and my installing a new backsplash, or removing hardware, or painting a cabinet, I'd feel an emotional snag. I'd connect to it through a random memory finding its way through the cracks of my soul. Nancy would stop and hold space for me. Her and Sam's ability to be empathetic is the stuff emotional intelligence is made from.

Soon enough, I was eager and brave enough to revisit my life in Hawaii with Darrell. I took off one day to drive around the island. I headed east. I stopped at the Hawaii Kai shopping area for lunch. I sat overlooking the boat harbor, in view of my Dad's old home on the bay. I remembered all the fun we had skiing, fishing, crabbing, and bringing friends with all their kids over to Dad's for sleepovers. I laughed thinking about the WWE kind of fake wrestling Darrell and my brothers, Dan, Kevin, and Josh performed and sometimes invoked our friends to join as part of our weekend amusement. And, of course, the little ones got in on the slow-motion flips and turns.

Knowing I had a long drive ahead, I collected my memories to continue on to the first home we purchased right before Brian had been born. It looked just as I remembered, but it mocked me somehow. It felt fake as if I were remembering someone else's story. I didn't linger, feeling unwelcome. Creeping round the bend of the Island, I stopped at Makapu'u Beach where we had taken our last family photo in Hawaii. Looking toward the lighthouse, a memory leaped into my mind about the argument Darrell and I had while getting ready for the photo shoot there. It was about who was supposed to pick up the flower haikus and leis. Neither of us did, and it made us late. I smiled remembering the silliness of that quarrel and was thankful that the angst had faded off our faces before the pictures were taken.

We tried hard to be successfully married in our twenties but still hadn't worked out how to give each other free air. It was a habit that didn't follow us forever as we matured and found corrective help for unrighteous expectations. I enjoyed that memory in the context of our growth. We eventually got over ourselves and stopped turning our desires (which may or may not be legitimate) into goals to change each other into our very own images. That behavior is plainly called rejection. I reflected on the privilege we had of falling in love over and over again as we learned to love more perfectly.

I left Makapuu Beach with a brief smile, content that the memory had found a new home in my heart or wherever those things are stored in the body. There was still no overwhelming emotion. I didn't mind. I continued weaving my way around the east end of the Island heading west. Suddenly uncomfortable in the air of silence, I decided to turn on the radio. It was in the middle of the song "It Must Have Been Love". The first lyrics I heard reminded me we were over now. Those words plowed down into my gut.

What the heck? I was just a few minutes before finding some comfort in memory and determined that was a sign of progress. A friend had told me at the funeral that one day memories would make me smile. Finally, it seemed true. But now, undulating anguish, accompanied by blinding tears, caused me to pull to the side of the road. I gave into it.

It *was* over. "We" had died. The song continued. The other lyrics poked holes too—like those that spoke of being tossed as easily as the wind blew. I felt the lines declaring time had run out. I heaved forward in my seat when reminded I will never be sheltered by his love; that line was especially visceral now that I had faced several threats alone. My hands trembled trying to turn off the radio, trying to stop more threatening words from pumping agony into the car. Even then, my thoughts took over where the lyrics left off.

As a couple, we had become all that I had wanted. Every good quality I saw in Darrell when we first met, he outpaced as he grew older. His sacrificial love was a beauty that swallowed every terrible agony we had ever faced. We found grace and renewal over and over for many well-worn years. Profound safety was the result. Cars whizzed by my de facto mourning chamber. I wanted the noise of the outside world to stop... to leave me be. Then the whizzing faded into a hallowed silence.

I suddenly felt that my soul tie with him was breaking, not that I hadn't felt it before, but Darrell was especially dead in that random moment... in the random dirt on the side of a random road. From seemingly nowhere, I saw Dad teaching me to burn the ends of a cut rope to seal its two frayed ends. I didn't know what to do with that image, but the implicit finality of its message—the fraying of us in my life—startled me back to the whizzing cars.

I uncoiled myself in the car and finished the drive, although only making it halfway around Oahu. Hot tears accompanied me until I reached the Like-Like Highway, where I cut through the mountain on my way back to my friends' house. By the time I reached Honolulu, I had left the tears behind. I couldn't cry even if I had wanted to. With a shrug, I allowed my curiosity to ward off any analysis or conclusions. Once back, I felt oddly satisfied to have endured the tsunami of emotion that came from the deep soul quake I hadn't properly anticipated.

I rode a few smaller waves of emotion during my time in Hawaii; but as the days passed, I sensed a new strength coming from the anticipation and, yes, the excitement about what each new day might bring. It was profound to feel strangely empowered. It was strange only because the intensity of the pain that randomly spun me in its gusts might have been disabling, as it had been over the past few months. But, it was not. I suspected and hoped that it meant I was adapting.

The redemptive quality of my mind changing, of being able to process memories, of a new bravery to embrace uncertainty, felt miraculous. Maybe this was my ultimate adventure, the one my mind had foreshadowed when I first landed. I dutifully visited the other homes we owned in Hawaii. They too felt impersonal without us. But, as I walked to the edge of our property in Waipahu from the park behind the house, I saw the roof first. A big smile landed on my face, remembering climbing onto it with our adult friends to watch shooting stars. Having those memories without pain went in my "adventure bag" with a wink. They fortunately fit neatly tucked next to the deeply emotional recollections. It was me, all me. And I liked me more and more in my unaccompanied world. I continued to explore.

The redemptive quality of my mind changing, of being able to process memories, of a new bravery to embrace uncertainty, felt miraculous.

As I left that last property, I began daydreaming like I was seeing into the innocence of us from those days. I recalled all that we had experienced there. I saw the children playing and laughing, the little parties we had hosted for them, Darrell fussing about with his flowers, planting the papaya and banana trees (still supplying fruit), and finding bugs and lizards with the kids. I saw myself happily preparing meals and serving family and friends. We learned to live in a rich community in that house and carried that value into our older lives together. I reveled at how alive those days were with purpose and how alive with promise our little family was in that world.

I couldn't stop thinking about my children in the next days after visiting our homes. The contrasts between who we were then and who we were now seemed stark. I thought of Brian's conversation with Darrell expressing his confusion over God's will and power to heal, perhaps wondering about God's existence at all. It summed up the apathy my children might be assimilating. I understood. I needed to reconcile it for myself. But it nevertheless grieved me that after leaving Hawaii all those years ago, all of us were hurled farther and farther from the simplicity and the purity of the world of promise we created in Hawaii. The experiences they had that touched their little souls as they grew up, were real. Could any of us recapture child-like faith in the world we had to traverse now?

How does one reconcile the indifference of this world with an all-powerful God, except to find a way to know they are not the same? I knew that was part of my solo journey to see that God was not indifferent even if the world was. It had to be each of my children's discovery too but they were hurting, and my own hurting pushed their pain deeper within. They were gallant to make their needs secondary to mine as they seemed to be doing, but I knew it was getting to be too much. They needed to not worry about me. That was one of the reasons I was in Hawaii—to give us all space.

I went to Waikiki one night to hear Hawaiian music, one of my playlist favorites, David Kahiapo. It was one of those openhanded moments to see what I could see, or rather feel what I could feel. Darrell knew David as they both had a heart for the plight of indigenous people. I knew him only through his music. As I sat there, listening to David's soothing songs, a couple got up to dance. I didn't like it. I left to walk the beach. Romance mockingly followed. It was everywhere, aided by twinkly lights wrapped around coconut trees, the smells of the ocean and plumeria flowers, and plenty of lovers enjoying themselves. I became annoyed and left thinking the night was a wash. The next time I went to hear David on the beach, I was with Sam and Nancy. Much better.

I arranged to stay at a retreat center in a lush valley, but on the first day a large local man in the cottage next to mine made a lewd comment. It put me on guard and took me out of any mediative or journaling zone, which I had hoped to savor. I never really slept perhaps because of the snoring, scary-lewd-man I heard through the wall separating our cottages. Another wash. But I took some great photos.

A friend invited Nancy and me to her cottage on the North Shore for a few days. The friend called me a mystery woman. I hadn't realized that I had a habit of wandering off without warning. But, she didn't mind since she too, had faced life-altering losses and grief. I appreciated that she extended me so much grace. Once at the cottage, the lull of the ocean waves, the sun, the turtles lounging on the beach, and my long walks along the shore had a sedative effect on my body. I sank into the sand outside the cottage and thought I would read. But nature's language seemed too important to add someone else's words. I listened. I slept. That's all.

One morning, I discovered a three-flippered sea turtle on the shore. It looked as if one of his front flippers had been bitten off recently. Some locals happened across it shortly after. We all postulated about a shark attack and about this creature's inability to get back into the ocean. The group jointly decided to help the turtle back into the surf (even though he probably needed a rest). An energetic and compassionate little girl, who named the turtle Sandy, was cheering, "You can do it, Sandy, you can do it." Her purity and love touched me deeply for the belief she possessed for this wounded creature. It was as if she were encouraging me too. She was an endorsement of the beauty that can be found in humanity.

I finally read that book I had tried to read before but couldn't. It was my first read since Darrell had passed—never mind that it was a very short book. This accomplishment was another feel-good moment. I could focus, which relieved a concern I developed about my mental capacities. I even took notes and felt inspired to write again. It felt like... me. I was ready to see friends and spend time with my family. The next thing I needed to do was spread my Dad's ashes on the islands as he had asked me to before he died. The box housing Dad was heavy and because I needed to carry it on the plane, I had wanted to lighten it by spreading some of Dad's ashes in Virginia first.

After dropping the box on my foot and breaking a toe, Jeffrey and I took my Dad's remains to the Atlantic Ocean to leave part of him there before I traveled to the Islands. We joked that he could meet up with me in Hawaii as we attempted a little memorial of sorts on the edge of a pier. It was cut short when a family appeared and were nearing us. So, with the bag of ashes in hand, I said good-bye to Dad quickly and began to pour the remaining part of him out. It was caught in the wind and flew in my face. I breathed it in, horrified. I did my best to cough Dad out while noticing most of what I had left in the Atlantic had first fallen on my shoe and the edge of the pier.

As the family approached, I squatted to brush Dad into the water. Jeffrey and I looked wide-eyed at each other, while the family was oblivious. We erupted in laughter on our way back to the car. Jeffrey made some witty comments about Grandpa still being challenging and making us clean up after him. Again. Yeah, it was Kevin's turn to take care of Dad.

My brother and sister-in-law, Missy, picked me up to drive us to the cemetery where my stepmother, Joyce, was buried. Missy brought gorgeous tropical flowers to honor them both. I brought Dad. We were going to pour a bit of Dad on Joyce's grave, but it was déjà vu. The planned ceremony was interrupted. A local couple was approaching to pay their respects to Joyce's deceased neighbor. Kevin quickly began to pour Dad out while Missy distracted the folks with her contagious charm. But chunks of bone poured out too. Now pieces of Dad stood out in relief against the grass. I felt a bit naughty as we tried to hide them from the neighboring family. I had not realized back in Virginia that Dad was still in chunks.

I chuckled at the juxtaposition of our intentional effort with the flippancy of another misadventure. The three of us took it in our stride and decided to take Dad to the bay, where his house was and leave the rest of him there. Dad, chunks and all, finally found his way back to Joyce and their home on the bay. I was glad to share this goodbye with my brother in a tangible way. It helped us both. I hadn't given my grief for Dad much thought after the memorial service we had hosted. But as proper goodbyes are supposed to go, even the unscripted and untimely ones, they help transfer bits of life from the "active file" to the safe place of acceptance.

Kevin, Missy, and I spent beautiful moments together, which included rich communication, entertainment, and sharing beautiful food at their lovely home and in the best restaurants. Their hospitality was extravagant. Their love was easy and their comfort as my family was deeply felt. It settled in as a nuanced personal awareness, a certain but different identity building within me. I felt normality swirling, making real life tangible.

I finished my trip doing touristy things. I went snorkeling several times and chartered a boat with twenty other people to swim with the turtles, ignoring the young crewman who assumed I was there just for the ride. To him I was apparently *not* like the rest of the younger passengers enjoying the adventure with lovers or friends. Never minding him, my fifty-nine-year-old-self jumped in before the rest of the tourists. I fixed him! Or not. I was, however, fixing myself... more and more. I wrote in my journal that it felt like I was connecting with who I had been while at the same time embracing the advent of becoming all that I could be. It felt healthy.

One of the last days in Hawaii was spent with my dear friend, Tracy, who had also been widowed way too early in life. We were easy friends but now having similar experiences with the sudden deaths of our husbands, our reconnection was life-giving. One day we planned to watch the sun set and go snorkeling at one of the lagoons in Ko'Olina. She had a friendly octopus to show me but instead found a sea slug, which promptly squirted her face with goo when she picked it up. We roared in the waves as our heads bobbed, hers a bit slimy.

As the sun was setting, I left her with another friend and weaved my way down a lush path for a better view. I sat by myself on a sea wall made of lava rocks. I was struck by the way the light sparkled and danced in the rippling water before the sun disappeared. It reminded me of the dappling light experience in England—whispering, leading, and inviting a response.

I LEAVE YOU JOY

left Hawaii having found a reprieve. The way memories are integrated after a loss is complicated since our loved ones are stored in different memory systems. To update those memories and lessen the threat the brain perceives from their absence, new memories need to be made.[15] I did that to a large degree, evidenced by a general sense of belonging in the world growing in me, especially after my trip. I wrote most of this book in the first few months back. I was ready to understand and process my losses and grief.

I took time to learn about the cognitive changes that widows and widowers experience and gave myself a break for the ones that

---

15   M.K. Shear, "Grief and Mourning Gone Awry: Pathway and Course of
     Complicated Grief," Dialogues Clinical Neuroscience. June 14(2):119-23. (2012)
     DOI:10.31887/DCNS.2012.14.2/mshear.

worried me.[16] I stopped having foreboding dreams about my safety, which meant I was harmonizing the past with the present, my conscience with my subconscious. I was eager to sort through more of Darrell's belongings, which were increasingly in my way. Sarah took me on a cruise in January 2022 as a gift for my 60th birthday, sailing out of New Orleans after first falling in love with the live jazz music that was everywhere. I was energized, content, and kind to myself. I was even having fun.

Then halfway through the writing process, things went wrong. Terribly wrong. I feared newly-gained progress would be eclipsed. I felt like Leonardo DiCaprio's character in *The Man In The Iron Mask,* who after tasting freedom was forcibly locked up again. I was like, "No, no, no, no, no!" Panic surged through my body.

So mocking were my circumstances that I wondered how I was ever going to finish the book and have anything promising to say. I had looked forward to meeting me in the last chapter, but the me I saw could not be presented to the world. What was I going to sound like: "Hamburger Lady" (from the English Band, Throbbing Gristle)? I could scarcely believe that some of the dangers of widowhood had come to outflank me as if I hadn't found hope, as if whatever peace I had found wasn't real. My body and mind didn't react well to a cascading event yelling its lasting consequences. My cortisol levels shot through the roof again. In unforgiving interludes, doubt for my survival hunted my peace.[17]

---

16 Biddle states that the neurological changes in widows is three times faster than married women. Biddle et al. "Associations of Widowhood and β-Amyloid With Cognitive Decline in Cognitively Unimpaired Older Adults" *JAMA.* 2020;3(2):e200121. doi:10.1001/jamanetworkopen.2020.0121

17 "Coping with trauma entails a period of appraisal of the threat and its possible implications. Expectations of danger and safety in certain circumstances may

I started having a repeated dream about my baby being taken from me, waking up terrified. A question plagued my mind, "What do I say in the last chapter—NEVER MIND?" It was all too fantastical to be believed. Dissociative behaviors were back, and I hated witnessing them in myself again.[18]

Perhaps I didn't need a Hollywood ending for my troubles, but I did expect diminishing feelings of real vulnerability to find their end. But in mid-2022, my days were lived squeezing the eyes of my soul shut in the desperation that I would find some way to recapture the confidence regained from the progress I had made. I found myself flipping from magical thinking (that the circumstance wasn't really as it appeared) to dumbing down my life just to survive. "I don't quit, not now, not after all the progress I just made," I told myself over and over. Yet, it felt like I was quitting to be void of the creative energy that had often animated my life, even in grim circumstances.

Nevertheless, this felt important. It brought articulation to an experience that seemed unfamiliar and to a motivation that conflicted with the values I held about living true. Once I could think about my reactions and recognize I was definitely in the double-minded-danger-zone, I knew that finding peace meant I'd have to add new values to the equation of my new unwelcomed prob-

---

be revised. Coping with loss requires a major modification of the memory systems that typically contain extensive information about the loved one. The finality and consequences of the loss must be assimilated and life goals and plans redefined without expectations of the loved one being included." Filip Dabergott (2021) The gendered widowhood effect and social mortality gap, Population Studies, DOI: 10.1080/00324728.2021.1892809

18 "Dissociation is a protective mechanism triggered when the brain researches maximum capacity to process input. When your resources are overwhelmed by things you can't control." Shulman (Audio Book, Chapter 5).

lem. I didn't know how to find them. I was in need of a change of mind and for the bravery that had been lost on me. I wanted to push this suffering away but knowing that effort hadn't helped anytime I tried, I let it be. I couldn't squirm my way out no matter.

> The expectations I had for myself felt as critical as an uncaring taskmaster.

The last couple years of processing helped me sort out the trauma of loss and gave me samples of possible peace. It was real and progressive. It felt strategic to say so; I couldn't deny it unless cynicism was going to have its complete way with me. But claiming I had made progress took all my strength, like jamming a securing rod into the face of a cliff from which I dangled. I was clinging for my life making these half-hearted proclamations but equally wondered if I had finally been mortally outplayed, not merely by outside forces but those inside? The expectations I had for myself felt as critical as an uncaring taskmaster.

To find myself falling short begged questions for which I didn't have answers. I stared them down, anyway, as they ravaged my soul, not in-your-face defiantly, but motionless and too tired of trying to obey their demands. It was one thing to know the unreasonable accusations of events and other people and sort out my reactions. I had managed to find the strength to discount those things—the things happening *to* me. Now it seemed that I was the problem. I couldn't find a playbook for integrating that reality. It sent my mind reeling, searching.

The event that triggered this steep dive into personal doubt was being targeted in an investment scam by someone I thought

I trusted but ended up being someone pretending to be the trust-worthy financial guru. Even though I was targeted for this scheme, (as widows often are), in my mind, it would be my fault if I couldn't pursue the dreams I had left—the ones keeping me alive. No matter how many of my friends and authorities sympathized, even telling their own stories of fraud, the situation stole my confidence. The financial consequences of losing personal funds were damaging, but not more than how I judged myself for being taken in by a lie and flailing about, trying to stop the bleeding.

The absolute worst of the condemnation raining down on me was thinking that the loss of my vitality would forfeit the example I wanted to leave for my children. The (imagined) disdain from them, along with losing my resources, were losses unimaginable to overcome. Would they see any rewards from my life of service and personal sacrifice or would they, in one fell swoop, discount all I had been and latch onto the cynicism I, too, was being tempted to absorb at wholesale value?

I mused through past generations and I thought about my protagonist, William Penn, in my historical story and his financial troubles. Some were from his being outright advantaged, some from being too trusting of others, and some from his own foolishness. When his children felt those consequences and saw the underbelly of both church and state, it made them reject their father's truest hopes for them. It was real and sad. I remembered those in history that decided it was futile to serve God.[19] I might not be exempt from this fate, blaming myself and God knows who else. My mind created the list.

_____

19   Malachi 3:5

Any flicker of hope about some unknown silver lining couldn't rouse me enough to find my courage. I observed my past fortitude from the island of skeptics living in my mind, as if I were watching the fading embers of a final SOS bonfire. I wanted to beg for intervention. Surely God knew all I had earnestly given, all our resources that had been sacrificed in ministry—it all played nasty tricks in my mind and exasperated the misery. I felt regret about all the sincere but nonsensical things we did to sacrifice for the church and for others. I hated thinking this way; I knew it was dangerously negative to do so. How could the idea of my selfless generosity now make me want excuses or tempt me to use it as collateral for bargaining?

Regrets are terribly wasteful but there they were, circling about like flies on a sweltering day. I was sickened that I could entertain these dimmest of thoughts. How could this be... me? But it was. I never thought I could be dark and now for a second time since Darrell passed, I was. I stayed in my room, no longer looking for better days to prove a thing. I didn't want anyone to see me. Dark days turned into months. It was a wonder I hadn't hit this kind of rock bottom before now, that it took me sixty years to feel this level of exposure. It made me miss the days that were purely grief and disappointment. Whatever I thought being lost felt like before, wasn't even close to this. The stakes could not be higher.

One day while still feeling utterly ruined, I pondered the dappling light experiences in England at Margaret Fox's home and on my hike in the Lake District. Were they merely my silly, wishful imagination for a victorious ending I might earn for my troubles? At the time, they gave me the imagery I needed to make hope and faith visceral. It was abstract and yet remarkably provoking, even when I was poker-faced with God in the early days of my widowhood. When I embraced the experience again from this new ugly vantage point and did the hard work of acknowledging the promise it had been to have had enough light for the moments as they came, a familiar question formed in my head. Could I answer the *even-if* question now? Could I trust that I could be vibrant once again even-if I made the worst mistake? So far, I couldn't. My dread informed me that I was stuck in the forbidden terrain of *what-ifs*. Not the kind that spurns invention but the kind that catastrophizes and braces itself for dangers it assumes is around every corner. I couldn't stay there. That's all I knew. What-ifs had to find a way to become even-ifs. That thought shifted my mind to at least peek out from hiding.

Without my handy self-sufficiency and from a great depth of abandonment, all my imagination could do was look back at my incredible blessings. They *were* real and substantial! It occurred to me that many of those bits of light that had kept me safe and moving forward had names. Names like Nancy and Bill... and so *very* many more. One by one, dozens and dozens of names danced through my mind like the dappling light had done in the Great Knott Wood—my family, friends, peers, doctors, authors I read, and the strangers who had shown me kindness. They were all those bits of light that gave me sight, hundreds of them over my lifetime. Tears of gratitude soaked my pillow. My mind journeyed more.

> It occurred to me that many of those bits of light that had kept me safe and moving forward had names.

I thought of my Native American friends, Brian, Fred, Dane, and Roy, who helped me at a critical point when I was utterly afraid, who compassionately said to me, "Now you know what it's like to be Native." Being marginalized and commodified as if people have no value is the worst humans can do to each other. My life's dream was that my work would address this terrible human habit. But now, I was the one who felt the extra fury of that evil and what havoc it wreaks on the psyche.

I thought of all I had learned in history and the people I had had the opportunity to know and sometimes help who had been victimized by something or someone. I felt the consequences of being used by those who freely manipulate the weak, vulnerable, and truly alone. These thoughts turned into travail, but strangely it was not for myself. It was for the vast human toll this terrible evil has perpetuated on the world. The children, the trafficked, the women, the widows, those in the margins, and those caught in evil wars were all targeted because someone had dehumanized them, used them as biofuel for their enrichment, and thought they could take what wasn't freely given.

I lamented with gut-wrenching grief. Suddenly I was one of those who groaned with creation about the imperfections of the world. This reflective mode went on for days before I opened my neglected Bible to Romans chapter eight. I read it with brand new insight. I understood the frustrations of creation that it speaks to and how they could be the doorway to liberation. To know personal freedom, we cannot be so dependent on this world, its outcomes, or resources—including the resource of self, which I suddenly saw as the two-faced mask I sometimes wore.

Liberation begins by deposing self (which includes self-pity as well as pride) and then believing that our promises are resident and bigger than ourselves or the effects of any other human being. That's tough and feels unfair when that very ask feels like accepting more loss but I knew my life's purpose could not be frantic flag-waving, as if to protect my ground. It was too late, anyway. Besides, it's no way to live. While the sin of being commodified belonged to someone else, and I had justly involved the authorities, my wholeness and peace could not be dependent on others or regaining what had been lost. In any case, my funds may not ever be returned, according to the lawyers I spoke to in Washington, D.C.

> Liberation begins by deposing self (which includes self-pity as well as pride) and then believing that our promises are resident and bigger than ourselves or the effects of any other human being.

So yes, the even-if question was critical to answer if I was going to be free. The effects of the humiliation I had vowed to avoid by being good and smart would destroy my future faster than losing my money to evil, calculating entities. The question this time was not like the ones I had already answered and found courage in doing so. It was not even-if my son was brain-injured, or even-if my husbands died, or, even-if people withdrew the funding I needed for my projects, or all the other even-ifs that challenged me to believe. Throughout life, my habit of answering the question reoriented me, forced me to grow and positioned me to find peace and strength. But now, the question was much more primordial. The question was even-if I had ruined everything myself? The phrase plowed through my mind over and over one day lying in my gloomy room, hiding. Yes. No. Maybe. I agonizingly shouted to the air, "I don't know!"

I felt deserving of the consequences and feared them as much (and perhaps even more) as I had feared trying to figure out how to live without my husbands. Yet, over the course of a few weeks, my curiosity caused me to consider that I might find a way to reconcile the inherent tension of my circumstance with my personhood, the things I still knew to be true about myself. It was a marvel that the earth hadn't opened up to swallow me, although I still skittishly walked around wondering if it might.

As my brain worked hard over the next weeks sorting my thoughts, feelings, and memories, I disciplined myself to reject doomsday thinking. I got out of my room. It took deliberation but I was doing it. I painted a piece of artwork (a marionette doll cutting herself free). I spent more time outdoors. I set aside the manuscript of this book, stayed away from the news, and watched countless episodes of *Wicked Tuna* and anything about space and the universe. Go Figure. Then, one unassuming day on a chilly morning in 2023, walking my dog near a lake, something came into focus in my mind's eye. I imagined one more beckoning light coming near. It had a name too—Mercy. It suddenly took my breath away to see myself standing in its light.

I realized Mercy had been mine all along, not in the begging-for-mercy kind of way I referred to in my introduction, but in the unruffled gift of it. The meadow I had mused about before became real; as I had imagined back in the Great Knott Wood, there were no shadows to dodge. It was not because a knight in shining armor came to rescue me. There was no restitution being made. No one found the perpetrators. My TV series hadn't been bought or pro-duced. I hadn't been sufficiently funded in my nonprofit again. No! There was nothing material to override the ruts in my mind, but I was jumping the tracks nonetheless, and it had nothing to do with previous strengths or privileges. I couldn't really explain it, only that I had been led to this revelation by the glimmers of light that dappled over time and in the bleakest moments of my life. I realized that when I had stayed in whatever light there had been, I had felt safe and present, even when I could barely see, even when darkness pressed me into smaller and smaller specks of it. That was true not once but many times in the last couple of years since Darrell's death. It was when I refused to be content with the smallest measure of it, that life became pitch black. And never more than this experience.

> I realized Mercy had been mine all along, not in the begging-for-mercy kind of way but in the unruffled gift of it.

I found a bench overlooking the lake to catch my breath—and to avoid having to be mindful of passersby since tears were streaming down my cheeks, even though I knew I wasn't ugly-crying. It seemed like that reduced state of being I had felt was now consumed in the transcendent and bright space I found myself in, a rip in time that opened life for me once again. I was like that young fifteen-year-old girl having my first encounter with unconditional love. But unlike that time when I couldn't comprehend my need for Mercy, I was matured by suffering and driven by shame. The sum of my life—especially all I experienced during the last couple of years—brought me to the edge of revelation, but Mercy brought me into the depths.

Even-if I had made a mistake, my belonging and the promises of rich life pouring over me now overtook the fear of losing myself.

I thought of Romans again. "Therefore, there is now no condemnation."[20] I felt it to my core. "This is incredible!" I whispered. This
was what my soul frustratingly sought, as if looking for a missing
something it never could describe, yet it was hiding in plain sight.
Running into Mercy shifted my personality. I didn't quite comprehend how or why, but what I did know was that my truest self was
going to be forever wrapped in Mercy. Elohi Chaseddi, the god of
my mercy.

Months passed. I knew it was real when the doubt that had
been chasing me couldn't land anymore. Like the words and attitude of someone who takes themselves too seriously, they were even
funny at times. Mistaken beliefs about forfeiting my future fell off
like leeches losing their suction. Scripture I had known leaped forward in my mind.[21] They were teeming with life. The verse about
being locked up until faith comes was so relevant. I *was* locked in
a mindset that blinded me. And then, just like that, I could see.

Challenging experiences require new depths of understanding and fresh insight. Just like my trying to find the relics of
Darrell's and my love wouldn't cut it for my present, so it is for
life-giving-beliefs. They have to be relevant in the most trying of
times, or they have no value. It's the space between one level of
understanding to the next that is so unsettling. It's like jumping
out of an airplane and your main parachute isn't enough and you
don't know if the secondary one will help, or even worse, you
don't know if you have a second chute at all. It's the not knowing that is always the scariest. For some reason this was the not-
knowing-ist time ever. And "not knowing" is where worn-out

---

20 Romans 8:1 (NIV)
21 Galatian 3:23, Romans 6:21, Hebrews 11, Romans 1:17, 1 Timothy 2:1

clichés and toxic positivity[22] are blatantly synthetic, especially the overly spiritualized kind that ignores what's really going on. It's good to see them as such.

Hope comes mysteriously to a life. This time in me, it was clearly birthed in meditation at my rock bottom that held my feet to the fire when all I wanted to do was run from it. I found new faith; it was accessed by Mercy. The peace it gave me was evidence that I was going to be okay. New confidence made the final arguments to condemning voices. Joy continued to erupt at random intervals while I continued to find myself smirking at circumstances which were still trying to be way too serious. I laughed spontaneously all by my lonesome self. That humor and joy was ever present with me, amazed me.

Mercy had touched me personally in my past, truly, but I also intellectualized it at times and perhaps used it as a sound bite in a spiritual context. Maybe I hadn't been an overt "sinner" in the obvious ways that people categorize bad behavior. Yet, I had been conditioned throughout my life to believe being strong and self-reliant was noble when a deeper look perhaps showed remnants of distrust, which is the root of mistaken behaviors of all sorts. So whether I was overtly "sinning," or not, it was all the same root. It distanced me from my truest self and from being able to fully grasp Mercy. But it didn't matter anymore. I knew it now, and it was changing me.

---

22   "While there are benefits to being optimistic and engaging in positive thinking toxic positivity rejects all difficult emotions in favor of a cheerful and often falsely-positive façade." Kendra Cherry "Toxic Positivity—"Why It's Harmful and What to Say Instead," *Verywell Mind* (2023) https://www.verywellmind.com/what-is-toxic-positivity

I was stronger. Seeing my weakness in light of Mercy made that curiously true. I fell in love with my humanity all over again and consciously became more connected to the world around me. I could write about this experience without regret. I needed to for other people's sakes. Triggers were disappearing. And that recognition was fun—to be minding my own business and suddenly realize that the thoughts that had harassed me before could not, not just about losing my money but many things. My friends commented that I was lighter. I felt rich in many ways and began to pity those who tried to take my life for they could never be as free as I was no matter how many luxuries they afforded themselves with my stolen funds.

While I realized I could never fully proof-text this deeply personal work or the light invading the shady corners of my mind, my body began reacting to it. It was literally like being bathed in the sun's glory on an island paradise, furnished with gentle trade winds to boot. And, I really did know what that felt like! No measure of brightness had been or was now unworthy of me, either, whether it was a pin light of truth or an entire meadow of it. It was all fully, 100% sufficient and one of the greatest legs of the adventure I had been on. I thought of the story of the women that was admired for her great faith because she acknowledged that even the crumbs that fall from the master's table were sufficient.[23] I really understood: not only were they sufficient but delicious.

It occurred to me that maybe this way of living—in dappling light—is what any of us ever get, and how it is supposed to be. Whether revelation is abundant or just enough for the next step

---

23   Matthew 15:26-28.

forward, it can be trusted, even in its uncomfortable demand to stay true. Suddenly, I knew how I was going to end this book, and it was perfect! It merged with all I had wanted to be and exceeded the hopes I had when I first started writing. I just didn't know that when I reached a seemingly dangerous bottom, there was a bit of ego in me that wished for an exception.

This was the ultimate terrible-beautiful adventure of suffering and becoming. Whatever I wrote in the introduction, after dark episode number one, was honestly true. After dark episode number two, it was reliably so but even more. While on the surface, it might seem unfair that my excursion through layers of loss had led me to a state of painful vulnerability (feelings of being unprotected, undervalued, and unsecured by every loss), what I gained in the end was empowering. Were my situations fateful or designed so that I could grow or "learn my lesson?" I don't believe that. Those who get stuck on such an idea end up with an uncompassionate worldview. But, can all things *work together* for our good and for our growth? Yes they can—that I believe![24]

My losses were my life yet, whether preventable or not, they did not create or void my identity, nor did they give me excuses or exceptions. Suffering came to me through life's harsh realities beyond my control... and also from the requirements of my own inner journey to wholeness no matter what cards I had been dealt. The bonus was realizing I hadn't forfeited my example to my children or for my work. It is exactly the example I wanted to leave them and anyone else caring to see it. When it occurred to me that the very ask being made of me to wrestle with all my uncertainties, all the even-ifs, and

---

24 Notice that I didn't say all things are good. They are not!

find hope, humility, and ultimately joy *was* and *is* exactly the same ask my work and my life's message had been making all along. All my questions and hesitations disappeared about how this story and my work could co-exist. The convergence happening in me was and continues to be profound. Just like Darrell's "struggle" was what I loved most about him, mine is what I love most about me. I win because of it. My children and work does too.

A much-loved quote by Florida Maxwell-Scott jettisoned forward in my mind. It says:

> *You need only claim the events of your life*
> *to make yourself yours.*
> *When you truly possess all*
> *you have been and done, which may take some time,*
> *you are fierce with reality.*[25]

It is a beautiful thing to have found myself more authentically mine by embracing all my life and finding no shame in pain or weakness, no identity in success or failure, and no circumstance able to (forever) impoverish my soul. It is what America and the world needs too: to claim *all* the events from our many stories, give ourselves no excuses, and not think something uncommon (though at times tragic) has happened.[26] If we did the hard work of owning our past and our present, the good bits and bobs as well as the unsightly

---

25   Florida Scott-Maxwell, The Measure of My Days, Enduring Celebration of Life and Aging (New York: Penguin Books, 1979), 42.

26   1 Peter 4:12

ones, it would give us the humility to see that personal healing and the world's healing is bound up in and for each other.

Otherwise, we think we are the exception, can make up the rules, have all the answers, or have all the justifications—but that helps no one. That kind of identity literally separates people from each other in that tricksy hierarchy-thingy that narrows or denies reality for others while lifting itself up. Not cool—not civil—not love!

I began this book with CS Lewis speaking to his pain, but I never finished the quote. I hadn't planned to, but I must. He says:

> But what is the good of telling you about my feelings?
> You know them already: they are the same as yours.
> I am not arguing that pain is not painful. Pain hurts.
> That is what the word means.
> I am only trying to show that the old Christian doctrine
> of being made 'perfect through suffering'
> [Hebrews 2:10] is not incredible.
> To prove it palatable is beyond my design.[27]

As I was coming to the end of this writing, I often pondered why joy has been so frequently equated with happiness when the path to finding it is anything but. That process of being perfected through suffering provides the opportunity to discover joy but it is not always happy since it is tied to the hard work of coming into wholeness. The more whole we become, the more joy flows

---

27 Lewis, The Problem of Pain, 93.

from a deep sense of wellbeing. It's spiritual in that sense.[28] Happiness is fun but it comes from the mundane—it comes and goes based on outward things, people, and events. But joy, when it is found, remains. It resounds loudest because of the condensing of life through pain and suffering. The best part is that it allows us to be present to ourselves and others, so we can live the authentic life most everyone I know longs for.

I do hope and sincerely pray as I continue my journey through widowhood and life that your bits of light will also lead you to joy, from one trusting moment to the next, until you are surrounded by a brightness that can change everything.[29] There is more. Keep going. I will too! We are in this together.

Darrell's words now ring out beautifully in my soul, "I leave you joy." He knew.

---

28   By definition spirituality is an overarching connection to a timeless something
     else. Even in Eastern religions wholeness and suffering are connected since its
     believed that struggles reveals the need to connect to something greater than self.
29   2 Corinthians 3:13, Romans 1:17

WORKS CITED

Biddle, Kelsey D et al. "Associations of Widowhood and β-Am-
    yloid With Cognitive Decline in Cognitively Unimpaired
    Older Adults." *JAMA Network Open.* Vol. 3,2 (2020) DOI:
    10.1001/jamanetworkopen.2020.0121

Bourne, Edmund J., PhD, *The Anxiety & Phobia Workbook,* Sixth
    Edition, Oakland: New Harbinger Publications, 2015.

Cherry, Kendra, MSEd, "Toxic Positivity—"Why It's Harmful
    and What to Say Instead," *Verywell Mind* (2023) https://www.
    verywellmind.com/what-is-toxic-positivity

Dabergott,Filip, "The Gendered Widowhood Effect and Social
    Mortality Gap," *Population Studies*, 76 (2021) 1-13. DOI: 10.
    1080/00324728.2021.1892809.

Giotakos, O, "Neurobiology of Emotional Trauma," *Psychiatriki*,
    Vol. 31, 2:162-171, April-June, 2020.

Good-Grief, "How to Create a Safe Space for Someone Who is Grieving," (2017) https://good-grief.org/wp-content/uploads/2017/04

Lewis, C.S. (1947). *The Problem With Pain.* New York: The McMillian Company,1947.

Mayo Clinic, *Complicated Grief,* 1998-2022 Mayo Foundation for Medical Education and Research (MFMER). Web access 07/23/2021, www.mayoclinic.com.

O'Conner, Mary Francis, *Grieving Brain: The Surprising Science of How We Learn From Love and Loss.* New York: Harper One, 2023.

Scott-Maxwell, Florida. *The Measure of My Days, Enduring Celebration of Life and Aging.* New York: Penguin Books,1979

Shear, MK., "Grief and Mourning Gone Awry: Pathway and Course of Complicated Grief," *Dialogues Clinical Neuroscience.* Jun;14(2):119-28.(2012) DOI: 10.31887/DCNS.2012.14.2/mshear.

Shulman, LM. (2018) *Before and After Loss. A Neurologist's Perspective on Loss, Grief, and Our Brain.* [Audio Book] Baltimore: John Hopkins University Press, 2018

ACKNOWLEDGMENTS

I need to thank those who were directly involved in the creation of this book: the staff at Morgan James publishing for their patient endurance balanced with their professional prodding to ensure that this book came to fruition. I especially want to thank David Hancock for taking a chance on this project.

I need to especially thank Quintin and Cheryl Frey who generously invested, financially and relationally, in this project. It was pretty incredible since it wasn't like I had made it to the finish line yet when they jumped on board. They were a huge reason I stayed on my feet.

I can't thank my editor, Carol Kay, enough for her expertise in helping me when my familiarity made my writing mistakes invisible. My reliving the story as I wrote made me susceptible to using the wrong tenses, as hard as I tried not to. Her respect of my voice and her quick turnaround impressed me.

I also can't forget those who read the earlier drafts and provided constructive critique, Deborah Strong (who coached me about writing). Tracy Yamamoto (who edited the earliest drafts and made me believe this project was important), Stephan Budasz (who spared me from embarrassing myself with my math and a few other typos), Sue Marrow (who read earliest versions and helped with naming chapters), and my heroic son, Jeffrey (whose critical eye was toughest of all). I don't know how he was able to do it as he was waylaid by memories and his own losses while reading it. Jeffrey, you are brilliant. I have to thank my mother, Laura Cox, for listening to me read to her. We laughed and cried together as I retold stories. She was an ever-ready supply of encouragement, reminding me of more events to tell. She would have had me write a novel. Nonetheless, it is wonderful to have a mom that only sees potential.

I have to thank my endorsers. I chose them to read my roughly edited ramblings and say something about them because they were ringside to my topsy-turvy process that became too fantastical to believe at times. They never once dissuaded me from writing. They could have cut their losses and told me to do the same, but they were my sherpas carrying my burden with me, without regret. They made me feel safe enough to write.

In addition to thanking Jeffrey, I have to thank my other children, Brain, Margarita, Chase, Sarah, and my grandchildren, Evangeline and Luca. They were and are the reason I write. They supported me in numerous beautiful ways, knowing I would find myself in words, eventually. My losses were theirs too, but they also had to make it through dangers of their own souls. They put on some heavy armor to do it. I pray each of them can take it off now and rest.

Lastly, I need to acknowledge my late step-mother, Joyce, who bought me my first laser printer when I was in my twenties and said, "Write!" when no one knew I could.

ABOUT THE
AUTHOR

L orrie Fields is an author, historian, and speaker based in Virginia Beach, VA. With over 20 years of public speaking experience—adeptly covering diverse topics from history to relationships. Lorrie had co-pastored a church with her husband, Darrell. She led a mission's school and traveled around the world with teams of all ages. She was also an interior designer for many years. But her gift of distilling complex information and history into meaningful ideas continues to be her passion whatever she is writing. A graduate of Regent University with a Bachelor of Arts in History, she is credited with scripts registered at The Writer's Guild of America. Additionally, Lorrie co-wrote a history book, *The Seed of a Nation*, with her second husband and spent the last years before his death creating a TV series based on her continued historical research.

Connecting:

To find out more and to connect with Lorrie go to:
www.lorriefields.com
www.facebook.com/lorrie.fields.7
www.instagram.com/@lorriemarrie

A free ebook edition is available with the purchase of this book.

To claim your free ebook edition:

1. Visit MorganJamesBOGO.com
2. Sign your name CLEARLY in the space
3. Complete the form and submit a photo of the entire copyright page
4. You or your friend can download the ebook to your preferred device

Morgan James
BOGO™

A **FREE** ebook edition is available for you
or a friend with the purchase of this print book.

CLEARLY SIGN YOUR NAME ABOVE

Instructions to claim your free ebook edition:
1. Visit MorganJamesBOGO.com
2. Sign your name CLEARLY in the space above
3. Complete the form and submit a photo
   of this entire page
4. You or your friend can download the ebook
   to your preferred device

Print & Digital Together Forever.

Snap a photo

Free ebook

Read anywhere

Printed in the USA
CPSIA information can be obtained
at www.ICGtesting.com
CBHW060421010624
9358CB00003B/19

9 781636 984582